Presbyterian Faith That Lives Today

Also by Donald K. McKim

The Church: Its Early Life

The Authority and Interpretation of the Bible: An Historical Approach (with Jack B. Rogers)

The Authoritative Word: Essays on the Nature of Scripture (editor)

Readings in Calvin's Theology (editor)

What Christians Believe about the Bible

A Guide to Contemporary Hermeneutics: Major Trends in Biblical Interpretation (editor)

How Karl Barth Changed My Mind (editor)

Ramism in William Perkins' Theology

Theological Turning Points: Major Issues in Christian Thought

Major Themes in the Reformed Tradition (editor)

Encyclopedia of the Reformed Faith (editor)

Kerygma: The Bible and Theology (4 volumes)

The Bible in Theology and Preaching

Westminster Dictionary of Theological Terms

God Never Forgets: Faith, Hope, and Alzheimer's Disease (editor)

Historical Handbook of Major Biblical Interpreters (editor)

Historical Dictionary of Reformed Churches (with Robert Benedetto and Darrell L. Guder)

Calvin's Institutes: Abridged Edition (editor)

Introducing the Reformed Faith: Biblical Revelation, Christian Tradition, Contemporary Significance

The Westminster Handbook to Reformed Theology (editor)

The Cambridge Companion to Martin Luther (editor)

Presbyterian Beliefs: A Brief Introduction

Presbyterian Questions, Presbyterian Answers

The Cambridge Companion to John Calvin (editor)

Calvin and the Bible (editor)

Historical Dictionary of Reformed Churches, 2nd ed. (with Robert Benedetto)

Dictionary of Major Biblical Interpreters (editor)

Ever a Vision: A Brief History of Pittsburgh Theological Seminary, 1959–2009

A Reformed Faith That Lives Today (Japanese translation)

More Presbyterian Questions, More Presbyterian Answers

A "Down and Dirty" Guide to Theology

Living into Lent

Coffee with Calvin: Daily Devotions

Presbyterian Faith
That Lives Today

DONALD K. MCKIM

Geneva Press
Louisville, Kentucky

First edition
Published by Geneva Press
Louisville, Kentucky

14 15 16 17 18 19 20 21 22 23—10 9 8 7 6 5 4 3 2 1

Book design by Erika Lundbom
Cover design by Dilu Nicholas

Library of Congress Cataloging-in-Publication Data

McKim, Donald K.
  The Presbyterian faith that lives today / Donald K. McKim. — First edition.
    pages cm
  ISBN 978-0-664-50334-5 (alk. paper)
  1. Presbyterian Church—Doctrines. 2. Reformed Church—Doctrines.
I. Title.
  BX9175.3.M355 2014
  230'.51—dc23

                                                                    2013049274

♾ The paper used in this publication meets the minimum requirements of the American National Standard for Information Sciences—Permanence of Paper for Printed Library Materials, ANSI Z39.48-1992

Most Geneva Press books are available at special quantity discounts when purchased in bulk by corporations, organizations, and special-interest groups. For more information, please e-mail SpecialSales@GenevaPress.com.

Suzanne Hawes McKim
May she be blessed with a living Christian faith

CONTENTS

PREFACE

I HAVE BEEN A LIFELONG PRESBYTERIAN. THE PRESBYTERIAN Church (U.S.A.) has been my denominational home, even as some of its immediate predecessor denominations have been part of my experience as well. My life in the church has enabled me to participate in various forms of ministry, most particularly in the largest sense as a theologian of the church. I have tried to provide theological resources for the Presbyterian Church and the Reformed family of churches as part of my overall work as a theologian. A number of the books I have written are focused on Reformed and Presbyterian topics.

This book is another one, written to provide theological understandings and nurturing for Presbyterians particularly. It doesn't cover everything there is to consider for Christian belief and Christian living, but it is a start. I offer it to the church in the spirit of St. Augustine's motto: Faith seeking understanding. "I believe in order to understand," said the great saint; that is the direction for who we are as Christians and our Christian lives.

The book originated with the Uemura lectures I presented for the Church of Christ in Japan a few years ago. LindaJo and I were graciously received throughout the presbyteries of this Reformed denomination, and it was an honor to be extended this opportunity to reflect together with Reformed Christians in Japan. I especially thank the Lecture Preparation Committee for the invitation to deliver these lectures as well as my friend, Dr. I. John Hesselink of Holland, Michigan, for suggesting my name to the committee. President Akira Miyoshi of Tokyo Theological Seminary and Rev. Yasumasa Sato gave us special help in preparing for and taking our journey. For all their wonderful kindnesses, LindaJo and I are especially grateful.

An earlier version of these lectures was translated into Japanese and published. This was also an honor.

For the interest of Geneva Press in publishing this volume, I am grateful. Thanks especially to David Dobson and Julie Tonini for their always excellent work and support.

My loving family brings blessings and joys to living. I thank my wonderful wife, LindaJo, for all her love, which encourages me along the way. Our sons and their families bring delight. Karl and Lauren share life with their energetic dog, Beatrice Arthur ("Bea"), and rabbit, Mr. Tipton. Stephen, Caroline, and Maddie have welcomed the birth of Suzanne Hawes McKim, to whom this book is dedicated. May Annie know the blessed joys of Christian faith and learn appreciatively from the Presbyterian tradition.

Donald K. McKim

Germantown, Tennessee
Reformation Day
October 31, 2013

INTRODUCTION

THIS BOOK IS FOR PRESBYTERIANS. I HOPE OTHERS BESIDES
Presbyterians will read it, but the book is for Presbyterians who want to know more about our Christian
faith. I have spent my life in the Presbyterian Church
(U.S.A.), so the book is specially written to those people in this communion. I offer a look at important theological beliefs we share as Presbyterians and what they
can mean for our lives. We share these beliefs with others in our Reformed family and with most Christians
throughout the world.

The Presbyterian Church (U.S.A.) is part of the
Reformed theological tradition. This tradition is rooted
in the sixteenth-century Protestant Reformation and is
associated with reformers such as Huldrych Zwingli,
Heinrich Bullinger, Martin Bucer, and most especially,

John Calvin. I have most often quoted Calvin in these pages. He was a leading voice, and his legacy to us endures. Other voices join the chorus. Presbyterians have inherited a rich theological heritage. We have many important theologians and confessional documents within our family circle. They speak with different accents and emphases, but they witness to a Reformed faith with significant theological emphases that, historically, have distinguished it from other Reformation theologies and ecclesiastical traditions as well as from Roman Catholic and Eastern Orthodox church traditions.

Since Presbyterians are part of a larger Reformed family, I sometimes refer specifically to a "Presbyterian" view, and sometimes to a "Reformed" view or to a "Presbyterian and Reformed view." These terms are meant to be basically synonymous. Both "Presbyterian" and "Reformed" are rightly used as adjectives. They are adjectives that modify the noun "Christian." We are "Presbyterian Christians" or "Reformed Christians." "Presbyterian" and "Reformed" are our ways of living and expressing our Christian faith. We are, first of all, Christians—disciples of Jesus Christ. This is our primary identity. We express this identity through our ecclesiastical and denominational traditions. Here in the United States, the Presbyterian Church (U.S.A.) is one Presbyterian denomination. There are others. All Presbyterians are part of the larger Reformed family, which includes churches that do not have "Presbyterian" as part of their names but that hold Reformed theological convictions in common with Presbyterians. Some examples are the United Church of Christ, the Reformed Church in America, and the Christian Reformed Church. The Reformed family has many branches in the United States and throughout the world. As we reflect theologically in relation to one denomination, we realize that there is a greater body—and a greater unity—that is represented by the terms "Presbyterian" and "Reformed."

This book is meant for those without formal theological education as well as seminary students and pastors. Much more documentation could have been provided, but I hope this has been written accessibly and can be read easily. The intention is to take a look at some important theological themes and how they have been understood and emphasized in Reformed and Presbyterian theology. These theological insights guide our churches and affect the whole of the church's life. The book does not try to prescribe answers to issues that the Presbyterian Church (U.S.A.) faces in these days. It does try to provide some foundational understandings that can broaden and deepen the faith of church members and provide theological nourishment for a Presbyterian faith that lives today.

Chapter 1

THE BIBLE

The Source of It All

WE BEGIN WITH THE BIBLE. FOR PRESBYTERIAN AND
Reformed Christians, the Bible is the source of it all.
The phrase says much. It focuses on "the Bible" and
the Bible as that which is the source of "all," of so
much for our Christian faith.

We are going back to basics for our Christian faith.
We are Christians. We know and love Jesus Christ. We
have dedicated our lives to serving God through Jesus
Christ by the power of the Holy Spirit. This is who we
are as persons, as Christians.

But when we probe further, or start thinking about
the reasons for this identity—or the ways in which we
know who God is, who Jesus Christ is, who the Holy
Spirit is—then we come back to the Bible. We acknowledge that the Bible is the source of our knowledge

of God; the Bible is the means by which we come to know Jesus Christ. The Bible is the continuing source for our understanding of what God wants us to do, in the church and in our Christian lives, by the work of the Holy Spirit among us and within us. So the Bible is basic—*very* basic. It is the source of our knowledge of the one God who has called us into lives of committed service and asked us to do God's work in this world as we live out the days we have been given on this earth. For Christians, the Bible is the source of it all.

Reformed Christians have been especially focused on the Bible. We believe Scripture is the means that God uses to communicate who God is and what God has done. The Bible is the unique source of our knowledge of God. We find God in Scripture, and God finds us in Scripture, as in no other book, as in no other place. So we recognize the special place the Bible holds as the way by which the message of the gospel of Jesus Christ is made known to us today. Throughout the writings of theologians in the Reformed tradition and confessions of faith by Reformed churches, emphasis is strong on the Bible as the authoritative source from which our Christian faith emerges.

THE NATURE OF THE BIBLE

How do we understand the nature of the Bible? This question is one of the most basic we have to ask. What we believe about the kind of book the Bible is has tremendous implications for a number of other dimensions of our Christian belief and lives of faith. We may not think of this point very much, but it's true. If you believe the Bible is a certain kind of document—given for a particular purpose and to be interpreted in a particular way—then your understandings of many other aspects of Christian faith are affected. The way you interpret the Bible reflects what you believe the nature of Scripture to be. If you believe the Bible is intended to convey certain types of information to contemporary people, you read the Scriptures with that type of focus. If you believe the Bible is a record of the religious experiences of some ancient people and that is about all, then you also interpret the Bible according to that type of conviction.[1]

So biblical interpretation is very much intertwined with our views about the nature of the Bible. In difficult passages or passages that seem unclear or contradictory, or perhaps not relevant for today—in all these kinds of approaches to interpretation, the place we come to as we interpret the Bible is greatly affected by our understanding of the kind of book it is. For this reason, we need to reflect on the nature of the Bible and understand what we are saying when we say the Bible is "the source of it all."

THE WORD OF GOD

One of the most important descriptions of the nature of Scripture, found throughout Reformed writings as well as in the Christian church more generally, is the description of Scripture as the Word of God. This point is captured in the opening words of the Second Helvetic Confession, written in 1566 by the Swiss reformer Heinrich Bullinger (1504–1575), which states, "We believe and confess the canonical Scriptures of the

holy prophets and apostles of both Testaments to be
the true Word of God, and to have sufficient authority
of themselves, not of men. For God himself spoke to
the fathers, prophets, apostles, and still speaks to us
through the Holy Scriptures."[2]

This confession affirms that the Bible, which consists
of the Old and New Testaments, is the "true Word of
God." This designation comes because it is through the
Scriptures that "God himself spoke." To say that "God
speaks" is to say "Word of God." God is the source or
the origination of the Scriptures. The Scriptures communicate God's very self. This self-communication of
God came to the biblical writers—"the fathers, prophets, and apostles"—but the confession goes on to say
that this communication continues now, into the present day, to us. God is continually communicated to us
"through the Scriptures."

In another place, the Reformer Bullinger wrote,
"We know very well that the Scripture is not called the
Word of God because of the human voice, the ink and
paper, or the printed letters (which all can be comprehended by the flesh), but because the meaning, which
speaks through the human voice or is written with pen
and ink on paper, is not originally from [humans], but
is God's word, will, and meaning."[3] Scripture as the
Word of God is more than words on a page; it is the
divine communication of God who through Scripture
communicates the divine will and purposes.

So to affirm Scripture as the Word of God is to
point to Scripture's origin as being with God and that
the Bible is the place we turn to know who God is and
what God has done.

THREE TERMS

Three terms describe dimensions of the Bible that can help shape our understandings of this claim about the Bible being the source of it all. These terms have emerged through the centuries in the church and are used by theologians to try to understand different aspects or facets of the nature of Scripture. These words offer ways of asking certain questions of the Bible and viewing the Bible in different lights in relation to the questions we are asking.

These terms can help us clarify certain aspects of Scripture and give us an appreciation for the gift that we have in Scripture. The Bible is—among many other things—a gift from God to us. It is God's way of providing for us a means that can become the source from which so much else flows. As we think on these things, we can be grateful for the gift of God that is the Scriptures themselves. No matter what we come to believe about particular aspects of Scripture—and our beliefs sometimes, sadly, divide Christians into differing groups—we can all confess our gratitude to God for the Bible as a source for us in understanding who God is, who we are, and how we can serve God in this world.

Revelation. The first term to consider is "revelation." When we hear that word, we may think of the New Testament book of Revelation. It is the last book in the New Testament, the last book in the whole Bible. The book of Revelation is mysterious, written with all kinds of graphic and strange images—beasts, battles, burning fires—and these can be very difficult to understand.

Yet the word "revelation" means an "uncovering," a "revealing," a "stripping away." That which has been hidden is now made known. A revelation provides a new knowledge, a new understanding, a new way of perceiving reality.

Theologically, we say "revelation" means that the God who is hidden has now been made known. The God who is beyond us has communicated with us. God has been revealed

Now that is a big idea, isn't it? To think that the eternal God, the God who is transcendent, beyond us, greater than us—greater than all else in the universe—has now been revealed or made known . . . can you think of any greater message than that? Revelation is the self-disclosure of the God whom we can never know by ourselves, on our own, by our human powers. To say that God is revealed is to make an astonishing claim! The claim is that we now have a knowledge or perception, an understanding of the eternal, divine God—which God has decided to make known to us limited, mortal, human beings.[4]

Historically the church has considered this astonishing idea of revelation in two dimensions. One is to ask: Is God revealed in nature? Is God revealed to the human mind? Can we know God by our own powers by observing what is around us or thinking about God in certain ways?

Christian theologians have come to differing conclusions in response to that question. Some, like Thomas Aquinas (1225–1274) in the Middle Ages, believed that certain logical arguments can convince us as rational creatures that there is a creator, a power behind all things that exist in the world. By following the logical proofs for the existence of God, we can know the reality of a divine power.

But Aquinas also knew that this wasn't enough. We need to know more than just that there is a power. If revelation is to be significant for us, we need to know the nature of that power, the character of that power behind all things. In short, we need to know who this God is.

This is why Christian theology, and our Presbyterian and Reformed view of Christian faith, has stressed the second dimension of God's revelation: God's revelation in Scripture. The Bible takes us where our reason cannot go. The Bible tells us not only that there is a God behind it all—the creator of all things—but the Bible is the means that God uses to reveal to us who God is.

We believe the Bible is God's self-revelation or self-communication. Through the Scriptures we learn the character, nature, and personality of God. This knowledge is not available to us from any other source. The Bible is a unique and an authoritative revelation of the God who created the heavens and the earth and then who has been involved with the creation, in the world, in human history, and particularly in the history of the people of God whom we know as the people of Israel and the people of God who make up the Christian church. The Bible tells us of a God who is revealed in history and who has called out a people within history to carry out God's purposes in and for the world that God created.

This, too, is an astonishing message—a message that leads to worship and praise! God has revealed who

God is through the Bible that has come to us. The great God has been revealed to human people. Imagine that!

This point is so astounding because "revelation" indicates that we have what we could never have gained by ourselves. We've been given the great gift of God, which is the knowledge of who God is and what God has done. We could never have gained that knowledge from any other source. We could never have climbed a ladder up to heaven, torn back the clouds, and peered into the face of the Creator God. Not us!

But the wonderful news of God's revelation is that we don't have to try. God has already done it. God has not made us ascend to heaven; God has descended to earth. God has communicated with us through other humans whom God used to write the Scriptures. We did not have to learn the language of God—"God-talk"—to be able to speak to God. Instead, God has learned our human languages and has communicated to us in the words of human beings that we can understand. This is the great gift of God's revelation.

We believe this revelation has come to us through the Scriptures of the Old and New Testaments. The Bible is the source of our knowledge of God, of God's revelation. The Bible is the means of God's self-communication. Whatever else we may believe about the Bible, this much is basic. The Bible is the gift God gives through which to make God known. So we celebrate the Bible as the source of it all. We honor and listen to Scripture in worship, in the church, and in our lives because we believe the Bible is God's revelation of the divine self. The Bible is God's gift of grace to us all.

Authority. A second word to help us understand the Bible as the source of it all is the word "authority." This term may seem rather flat, or perhaps even scary. We may not like to think of authority in our lives, since that brings up images of people with power over us who try to make us do what they want us to do instead of what we ourselves want to do.

In the church we speak of the "authority of Scripture." Christians have understood this term in different ways. It is used to describe the way we believe God's revelation—found in and through the Bible—becomes real for us, in the here and now. "Authority" is a way of indicating that we as Christians are recognizing who God is and what God has done, and we are responding to this message that God has been and is active in the world through Israel, through Jesus Christ.

Revealed in Scripture is the story of this God who has created the world and who has been at work within the world. Every biblical book conveys this message. God has been at work in this world, seeking to carry out the purposes of love—for the creation and for the people God made and who are created in the "image of God." People reject this love from God; they hide from it and they live lives without regard to what God wants, which the Bible calls "sin." Sin is the story of humanity, the story of each one of us.

Yet, in the midst of this sin, God does not close us down. God does not come in wrath and vengeance to make us pay for the results of all we have done that is contrary to God's will for us. No, the astonishing story of the Bible is that this God of love has loved us and continues to love us! The proof of this amazing love is that God sent the Son of God, Jesus Christ, into the world to live and die and be raised again so that the relationship with God that our sin has broken can now be restored and life can begin for us anew.

By faith we receive the gift of God's love in Jesus Christ in his life and death and resurrection. By the power of the Holy Spirit we believe this message of God's love in Christ, and we become disciples of Christ—"Christians," "little Christs"—in seeking now to live in obedience to God's Word and will for us and in service to the God we love in Christ, in this world. So the message of God's revelation in Scripture is very simple: God created the world, humans messed it up by sinning, and God has come to set things right in Jesus Christ.

We know the nature of this God and what God has done, particularly in Jesus Christ, through the Scripture, God's revelation. So we say the Scriptures have authority for us, in the church and in our lives. We acknowledge the unique message of the Bible and affirm that this message is the message by which our lives will be lived. We confess Jesus Christ as our Lord and Savior. Since we know Jesus Christ only through the Scriptures, we confess as well that the Bible is the source of it all for us. The Bible is the authority for our lives, since it is through the Scriptures that we come to know Jesus Christ and through them we know the message of the salvation that God has given to us in and through Christ. Martin Luther said that the Bible is "the manger in which Christ lies."[5]

We say the Bible is our authority because the message of God's love in Jesus Christ is made known to us through the Bible. We acknowledge this authority by also confessing that we want to live on the basis of this love that the Scriptures of the Old and New Testament convey to us. The Scriptures have authority for us in the church since they are the *locus* or the place where God is revealed. By acknowledging the Bible as God's authoritative word, we are aligning ourselves, by faith, with the God who is revealed in Scripture and who calls us to worship and serve Christ in this world.

The Bible is God's revelation. The Bible has authority for us in the church and in our lives.

Inspiration. One more term is important for us in understanding what we mean when we say that the Bible is the source of it all. That word is "inspiration."

As Presbyterian Christians, we say that God is revealed through the Scriptures, that the Scriptures have authority for us; we also say that the Bible is "inspired by God." Two biblical texts are important here. Second Timothy 3:16–17 says, "All Scripture is inspired by God and is useful for teaching, for reproof, for correction, and for training in righteousness, so that everyone who belongs to God may be proficient, equipped for every good work." The Holy Spirit inspires Scripture to be "useful." Scripture has a function to carry out, and that function is to equip "everyone who belongs to God" to be "equipped for every good work." The inspiration of Scripture is the work of the Holy Spirit.

A second text is 2 Peter 1:21, which says that "no prophecy ever came by human will, but men and women moved by the Holy Spirit spoke from God." The Holy Spirit used human beings to speak God's Word. The Spirit worked in and through real, live human beings and their personalities. Inspiration is both a divine and human activity.

The inspiration of Scripture is a way of confessing that we believe the Bible is a unique document, unlike all others. We believe God used humans to communicate God's message. How can this be? How can the great God condescend and accommodate the message of God to the world through humans?

To be honest, we don't know the answer to the how question. How can God do this? Actually, how can God do anything? We're humans, we're limited and finite—we can never know how the infinite, holy God can do something!

But we confess in the church that we believe God *has* done this. God has used human beings to communicate God's unique and authoritative message to us through the Scriptures. The way we confess this conviction is to say that we believe in the "inspiration of Scripture" or that the biblical writers were "inspired" as they conveyed God's Word or message in writing.

The word "inspired" can mean a lot of different things. We say a great work of art is "inspired," or that a great musical performance is "inspiring." A sports team that comes from behind to win in the last minutes of a game is "inspired." But the church has said the inspiration of Scripture is unique. The church believes that God has spoken through the writers of the Bible in a way that God has not spoken anywhere else.

How is this possible? We don't know. We do not know how God can work in and through the personalities of human writers to convey what God wants to convey. Inspiration is a mystery, just as revelation itself is a mystery. But it is an experienced reality just the same. God the communicator has desired to communicate a message—we call it the "gospel" or "good news." God wants us to respond to this message, so God has graciously chosen to use human beings to be the bearers of this message. God has used human beings and their language to say what God wants conveyed. In the Bible, God speaks as nowhere else.

Though we confess that the Scriptures are inspired, there are differing ways to understand the nature of this inspiration and what it means. To be honest, this issue poses difficulties between Christians. In Reformed churches, for example, there are at least five ways of understanding the inspiration of Scripture and its implications. These ways were explored in a Task Force on Biblical Authority and Interpretation report from the former United Presbyterian Church in the U.S.A. in 1982.[6]

First, some Reformed Christians believe that the Bible is merely a record of the moral and religious experiences of Hebrews and Christians. Inspiration then occurs only as people read the Bible and are inspired to live more loving and just lives.

Second, some Reformed Christians believe that portions of the Bible, including some of its theological and ethical positions, may not be the inspired Word of God. The parts of the Bible that convey moral or ethical or theological viewpoints that we believe are not consistent with the rest of the Bible are not regarded as inspired by God.

These two viewpoints, we can say, emphasize the human dimension of Scripture. Humans write what they write, and it may or may not be inspired or regarded as the Word of God.

On the other end of the spectrum, in the third place, some Reformed Christians believe that the Bible, though written by individuals, has been so controlled by the Holy Spirit that it is without error in all it teaches in matters of science and history as well as in matters of theology. This model sees the Bible as a book of inerrant facts—that no errors of any kind appear in the Scriptures. This viewpoint emphasizes almost exclusively the divine dimension of Scripture. Since the Bible is God's Word and God cannot lie, therefore the Bible cannot lie.

Between these extremes are two other viewpoints. The fourth position can be characterized as the Bible being a witness to Christ. In this view, the Bible, though written by individuals and reflecting their personalities, has been so controlled by the Holy Spirit that it is trustworthy in all it teaches in matters of theology and ethics, but not necessarily in matters of science and history. As one encounters the Christ of the Scriptures by faith through the Holy Spirit, one encounters an inspiration within oneself.

Finally, the fifth position that Reformed Christians hold is the one that is dominant in the Presbyterian Church (U.S.A.). In this view, inspiration is best understood by recognizing the entire Bible simultaneously as both the inspired Word of God and a thoroughly human document. The focus of this view is that the Bible is a book with a divine message in human thought forms. God uses human writers with their own limitations and personalities to communicate a message that transcends cultures. To understand this divine message, we need to pay the closest possible attention to human words and the contexts in which they are written. God inspired the writers of Scripture, mysteriously being able to work through their lives and personalities and writings with all their limitations to speak the Word of God through what we have today as our Bible.

These five views about the nature of the inspiration of the Bible mean that we have a variety of ways of understanding the nature of Scripture and its appropriate interpretation within Presbyterian and Reformed traditions. All the viewpoints acknowledge the Bible is somehow special or unique. The viewpoints vary on the ways in which they understand the nature of this uniqueness and what that uniqueness means for interpreting the Bible as a whole as well as in individual biblical passages.

WORD AND SPIRIT

Historically and classically, the Presbyterian and Reformed tradition has recognized the Bible as God's inspired, authoritative revelation. But to acknowledge the Bible in this way comes by the work of the Holy Spirit. The Spirit inspired the biblical writers in mysterious ways. The Spirit also illuminates those who read the Scriptures. It is the Spirit who witnesses to the Bible as the Word of God, just as the Spirit also witnesses to Jesus Christ as our Lord and Savior. We come to know and recognize the Bible as God's revelation, as being authoritative, and as being inspired by the work of the Holy Spirit. Word and Spirit are inextricably bound up together. The Spirit, in addition to inspiring the Word and illuminating our hearts and minds to recognize the Word, also helps us interpret the Word. The Holy Spirit of God leads us to understand what God's Word is saying to us and what the meaning of God's Word is for our lives, every day. The Holy Spirit makes the Word of God come alive for us.

The internal witness of the Holy Spirit is necessary, according to the Reformed tradition, to enable us to recognize Scripture as God's Word. John Calvin (1509–1564) wrote, "The Word will not find acceptance in men's hearts before it is sealed by the inward testimony of the Spirit. The same Spirit, therefore, who has spoken through the mouths of the prophets must penetrate into our hearts to persuade us that they faithfully proclaimed what had been divinely commanded."[7] We come to confess Scripture as the Word of God, as we confess Jesus Christ as Lord and Savior—not by our own intellects or reasoning powers but by the witness or testimony of the Holy Spirit in our hearts and minds.

THE BIBLE: THE SOURCE OF IT ALL

So where are we in all of this? The differing views of the inspiration of Scripture and various models of the authority of the Bible have practical consequences for us as Christians, and particularly as Presbyterian Christians. Many of the past and present controversies we have in the church can be traced back to these different ways of perceiving the nature of Scripture and the means of its appropriate interpretation.

Positively, however, we can affirm that for us as Presbyterian Christians, the Bible is the source of it all. Making that statement does not solve all our problems. There are many dimensions related to Scripture that need to be explored to gain further clarity about what we believe about the Bible. But to affirm that the Bible is the source of it all unites us with Christians in traditions other than the Reformed and Presbyterian. This confession unites us with other Christians who recognize the Bible as

-   the revelation or self-communication of God,
-   the authority for the church and for our individual lives, and
-   inspired by God to convey God's word to us in a way that we do not find in any other source.

As we live as Presbyterians in our churches, we can emphasize what unites us with other Christians. The more we study the Scriptures together, the more we listen and pray to God for the guidance of the Holy Spirit, the more we turn to the Scriptures to instruct us in what to believe and how to live—the more the Bible will take a central place in our lives. Our faith will live by nourishment from the Word. The Bible as the source of it all will become even more valued and treasured in our lives.

Chapter 2

THE GOD WHO CREATES AND PROVIDES

THE BIBLE, WHICH CONVEYS GOD'S DIVINE REVELATION OR self-communication to us, begins with the astonishing statement that "in the beginning God created the heavens and the earth" (Gen. 1:1 RSV; cf. Acts 17:24; Rev. 4:11). Right from the start we are introduced to God as creator. The rest of the Scriptures assume this reality. God is the one who is behind it all, who brought all things into existence, who is the "creator of all things visible and invisible," all things "seen and unseen," as the ancient creeds say. We can hardly think of a more comprehensive claim than that!

But the Bible also has much more to say about God. The God who is creator is also the one who provides for the creation. The Bible, the early church, and our

Reformed tradition affirm this point very strongly. If God had only created the world and then backed away—not upheld it by divine power—what would have happened? The world would have fallen back into the chaos that was there at the beginning. The whole creation would have collapsed. So it is important for the church and for Christian belief to maintain that the God who creates also provides. This God who brought all things into being now continues—through all the centuries—to uphold and support the creation by a power that maintains life and stability through the entire created universe.

Both dimensions are important. They are both supported by the Scriptures of the Old and New Testaments, which affirm God's creative power and God's sustaining power. No rival gods were present at the point of creation—other gods who had the same power as the one, true God, who is the God of Israel and the God of our Lord Jesus Christ. This God is the one and only, the true God.

God created all things out of nothing. Theologians call this "creation *ex nihilo*." God did not use what was already present in the universe to build or construct what was to come. There was no preexistent matter that God chose to use to bring into existence that which became the universe as we know it. Instead, as the book of Hebrews puts it, "By faith we understand that the worlds were prepared by the word of God, so that what is seen was made from things that are not visible," or "what is seen was not made out of visible things" (Heb. 11:3 plus variant).

Confessing God as the creator of all things, visible and invisible, and God as creator *ex nihilo* (out of nothing) affirms God as the sovereign Lord, the unique and only creator of the universe. Confessing God in this manner is to acknowledge God's supreme Lordship and sovereignty and God's place as the supreme creator of all. The Second Helvetic Confession (1566) reads, "This good and almighty God created all things, both visible and invisible, by his co-eternal Word, and preserves them by his co-eternal Spirit, as David testified when he said: 'By the word of the Lord the heavens were made, and all their host by the breath of his mouth.'"[1]

THE TRIUNE GOD

This reference from the Second Helvetic Confession points us also to something that is very important. Our Reformed tradition, as we find it expressed by theologians and in the confessions of faith that have emerged from the days of the Protestant Reformation in the sixteenth century, has confessed our faith in the triune God. We join with other Christians in the ecumenical church in confessing our faith in the Trinity. God is one God who is eternally three persons. The church believes in one God in three persons who lives and works in different ways at the same time. This concept has many dimensions, but we need to recognize the Trinity as a starting point for our understanding of God.

One God. From the time of the New Testament, Christians have believed in one God: the God of Israel who is revealed in the Hebrew Scriptures as the creator of all things and as the God who enters into a covenant with Abraham and Sarah (Gen. 12:1–3). This God called Moses and liberated the people of Israel from slavery in Egypt (Exod. 14–15) and entered into a covenant with the nation at Mount Sinai by giving the Ten Commandments (Exod. 20) as guides for living in the relationship God desires to have with the covenant community. This God spoke through the prophets, calling the people to covenant faithfulness and obedience. God promised a Messiah and to enter into a "new covenant" where the law of God will be written on the hearts of women and men (Jer. 31:31–34).

This one God who did all these things is the God who also sent Jesus Christ into the world as the Messiah, as the one through whom God has now enacted the "new covenant" that is sealed in the body and blood of Jesus Christ (1 Cor. 11:23–26). Jesus Christ is God's "only Son" who was given "so that everyone who believes in him may not perish but may have eternal life" (John 3:16). God desires to save the world through him (John 3:17).

Those who are followers of Jesus Christ, his disciples, believe that the God of Israel is the "God and Father of the Lord Jesus" (2 Cor. 11:31; Eph. 1:3). The God to whom Jesus prayed was the God of Israel. This God is one, a basic confession of the Jewish faith, going all the way back to the famous *Shema* in the book of Deuteronomy: "Hear, O Israel: The LORD is our God, the LORD alone" (Deut. 6:4; see Deut. 6:4–9). The apostle Paul proclaimed, "Yet for us there is one God, the Father, from whom are all things and for whom we exist, and one Lord, Jesus Christ, through

whom are all things and through whom we exist"
(1 Cor. 8:6).

So early Christians and the Christian church as it
developed in the early centuries affirmed that we believe
in and worship one God, who is the God of Israel.

Father, Son, and Holy Spirit. Other dimensions also
emerged. Early Christians maintained that this God is
now known in three ways: as Father, as Son, and as the
Holy Spirit. Each of these realities is a way of knowing
the one God. In some New Testament passages these
three are linked together. Most famously, perhaps,
they are joined in the benediction we frequently use in
churches from Paul's second letter to the Corinthians:
"The grace of the Lord Jesus Christ, the love of God,
and the communion of the Holy Spirit be with all of
you" (2 Cor. 13:13). Father, Son, and Holy Spirit are
mentioned simultaneously, indicating the conviction of
Paul that the one God is known at the same time as
Father, Son, and Holy Spirit.

The Distinctions of the Persons. A third element also
arose from the biblical materials in the early Christian
era: the Father, Son, and Holy Spirit are each distinct
from each other. The New Testament writings show
each of the three carrying out different works throughout human history. In the story of salvation, for example, the three work in distinct ways: God the Father
"sends" the Son into the world that we may have eternal life (John 3:16). But no one can confess the truth
of this reality unless the Holy Spirit enables that confession. As Paul said, "No one can say 'Jesus is Lord'
except by the Holy Spirit" (1 Cor. 12:3). Father, Son,

and Holy Spirit each have distinct ways of working in the world and for Christian salvation.

These basic directions were developed much further in the early centuries of the Christian church when the church and its theologians struggled to make sense of the New Testament materials and to articulate an understanding of who God is. The many zigs and zags of this story can be read in a number of places.[2] Three main kinds of issues had to be decided, and they can be captured in three words: unity, equality, and distinction.

- Is God "one God"? Is there an essential unity to the God whom Christians worship?
- Is there equality among the three: Father, Son, and Holy Spirit? Are they all fully and equally God?
- Can we recognize the distinctions among the three? Do we perceive that Father, Son, and Holy Spirit each have a unique personality or personhood and that they each carry out distinctive tasks or functions?

These three issues were the basics with which the Christian church had to deal as it hammered out the doctrine of the Trinity.

One God in Three Persons. In the end, the Christian doctrine of the Trinity emerged as Christians confessed that we believe in "one God in three persons." Father, Son, and Holy Spirit are all fully and equally God. They share the same "substance" (Gr. *ousia*; Lat. *substantia*), as the theologians put it, using an important term from

Greek philosophy. They are eternal and are united by the bond of love among them. Each is fully God, and each at the same time is a unique person or individual. They are "one in three" and "three in one" or "triune." There is a "trinity" *and* a "unity": unity, equality, and distinction.

This basic Christian conviction is expressed throughout Reformed confessional documents from the earliest period until later. The Tetrapolitan Confession (1530) says, "The Holy Trinity—viz. that God the Father, the Son and the Holy Ghost is one in substance, and admits no distinction other than of persons."[3] The First Helvetic Confession of Faith (1536) says, "Concerning God, we hold that there is one only, true, living and almighty God, one in essence, threefold according to the persons."[4] In the twentieth century, the "Brief Statement of Faith" of the Presbyterian Church (U.S.A.) stated,

In life and in death we belong to God.
Through the grace of our Lord Jesus Christ,
the love of God,
and the communion of the Holy Spirit,
we trust in the one triune God, the Holy One of Israel,
whom alone we worship and serve.[5]

We believe in the triune God: Father, Son, and Holy Spirit.

THE PERSONAL GOD

Our Reformed, Presbyterian, and Christian belief in the Trinity can sound rather distant or dry—without life or vitality. Theological terms like "trinity" and "substance" and "person" are necessary to witness to the realities we find in Scripture about who God is. But these terms, or the theological formulations, do not provide the whole picture or tell the entire story. Reformed theology affirms that we worship and serve a very personal God, the God about whose personality we learn in the Bible, as God's revelation or self-communication.

As we think of God in today's world, we need to recognize that God is not distant, aloof, or removed from the world. We recognize God as the creator of the universe and all things and see that God continues to provide for the creation. But we also have to realize that this personal God is intimately concerned with the creation and especially the persons who are part of the divine creation.

Theologians have spoken of the "attributes" of God. These are characteristics of God—what we can say about God that is true. These attributes are often drawn from the language of Western philosophy. They express truths about a supreme being. But Christian theology uses this language to try to say something true and significant about the God of Israel who is also the God and Father of our Lord Jesus Christ. We get a flavor of this from the definition of God in the Westminster Confession of Faith of 1647.

Q. 7. What is God?
A. God is a Spirit, in and of himself infinite in being, glory, blessedness, and perfection; all-sufficient, eternal, unchangeable, incomprehensible, everywhere present, almighty; knowing all things, most wise, most holy, most just, most merciful, and gracious, long-suffering, and abundant in goodness and truth.[6]

Each of the attributes here reflects a biblical understanding, and each constitutes a part of our understanding of who God is. All these attributes point to God's greatness, God's supremacy, and God's priority in relation to all else that exists.

But a different tone is struck in the Heidelberg Catechism (1563) when it asks,

> **Q. 26. What do you believe when you say: "I believe in God the Father Almighty, Maker of heaven and earth"?**
> A. That the eternal Father of our Lord Jesus Christ, who out of nothing created heaven and earth with all that is in them, who also upholds and governs them by his eternal counsel and providence, is for the sake of Christ his Son my God and my Father. I trust in him so completely that I have no doubt that he will provide me with all things necessary for body and soul. Moreover, whatever evil he sends upon me in this troubled life he will turn to my good, for he is able to do it, being almighty God, and is determined to do it, being a faithful Father.[7]

This approach is much more personal. It does not list a collection of attributes or characteristics as a way of describing the most important things to say about God. Here the description of what one believes about the nature of God is linked to the activities of a loving, parental God in providing for the comfort and relief of the Christian believer.

As a central way of understanding who God is, this focus on love breathes through the Scriptures. The psalms and the prophets proclaim it. The disciples and followers of Jesus Christ in the early church experienced it. Indeed, we recognize Jesus Christ as the proof of the divine love for us, as Paul writes in Romans 5:8. When we look to Jesus Christ, as the Son of God who came into the world to save sinners, we see this proof focused in a person. Writing on 1 John 4:9, "God's love was revealed among us in this way: God sent his only Son into the world so that we might live through him," John Calvin wrote:

> But here the apostle chooses the chief example which transcends everything else. For it was not only the infinite love of God which did not spare His own Son, that by His death He might restore us to life, but it was a more than wonderful goodness which ought to ravish our minds with amazement. Christ is such a shining and remarkable proof of the divine love toward us that, whenever we look to Him, He clearly confirms to us the doctrine that God is love.[8]

Of course, the Bible describes God in many other ways as well. But if we focus on one that can embrace all the rest, we can do no better than to say, as did the writer of 1 John, "God is love" (4:8).

GOD THE CREATOR

God's love is seen in Jesus Christ, who is also God's Word (John 1:1), and through him, according to the writer of the book of Hebrews, "also created the worlds" (Heb. 1:2). Recognizing the triune nature of God has led theologians to say that the act of one member of the divine Godhead is the act of the whole Godhead, or Trinity. God is one; the actions of any of the three persons of the Trinity constitute the action of God—and thus of all three persons: Father, Son, and

Holy Spirit. Calvin noted that "it is a usual manner of speaking to call the Father the Creator: and what is added in some passages—by Wisdom (Prov. 8.27) or by the Word (John 1.3), or by the Son (Col. 1.16)— has the same force as if Wisdom itself were named as Creator."[9] The contemporary theologian Jürgen Moltmann put it this way:

> The Christian doctrine of creation takes its impress from the revelation of Christ and the experience of the Spirit. The One who sends the Son and the Spirit is the Creator—the Father. The One who gathers the world under his liberating lordship, and redeems it, is the Word of creation—the Son. The One who gives life to the world and allows it to participate in God's eternal life is the creative Energy—the Spirit. The Father is the creating origin of creation, the Son its shaping origin, and the Spirit its life-giving origin. Creation exists in the Spirit, is molded by the Son and is created by the Father. It is therefore from God, through God and in God.[10]

Two implications of God the creator stand out.

All Creation Is God's. If God is the creator of all and creation is "from God, through God and in God," then all creation is God's. As the psalmist proclaimed, "The earth is the LORD's and all that is in it, the world, and those who live in it" (Ps. 24:1). The world around us, the natural world, belongs to God. Our environment is the creation of God and subject to God's will. Humans, as part of the creation, also created by God, have responsibilities to use the environment given to us for God's purposes and God's glory.

"Stewardship" is a term sometimes used to describe human responsibilities for the environment. We are to be good stewards or caretakers of what God has given us in the natural world to receive and enjoy. Our use of the world's resources should be for God's purposes, not our own. While humans may stand over nature, in that we have power by virtue of our humanity, we are also under God. God is the one who has given humanity all good gifts. We are to use the good creation according to the will of God—over nature, but under God. Our stewardship is our wise use of the earth's resources for the sake of God's concerns about this world—its future and its people. The doctrine of creation is then a powerful push toward a wise and responsible ecology of the creation. When God originally created the world, the Scripture says that God looked upon everything God had made and "it was very good" (Gen. 1:31). Our task today, living responsibly in our Reformed faith, is to live out God's will in using with wisdom and responsibility the resources we have been given.

Humanity as Created by God. A second implication of God the creator is that humans are the creation of God as well. Humanity is created by God and is thus inextricably linked to God, our creator.

The creation narratives in the book of Genesis move in this direction. God created Adam and Eve, representatives of the whole human family that has come afterward. The first couple enjoyed blessed communion and communication with God in the Garden of Eden, in paradise. They had a relationship with God that was unblocked by any internal or external force. They were created in the "image" of God (Lat. *imago Dei*; Gen. 1:27). Among all the many things that term can mean, one is that humans are "to image" God. We are to be God's representatives in the world, to reflect God's character and likeness, because God is our creator. Our lives belong to our creator, to God. We are to live in relationship with God, as was intended in the story of Adam and Eve. Our lives are not our own.

But we know that, according to the Bible, the creation of our first parents in Genesis 1—intended to enjoy a perfect relationship with God—was spoiled by human sin. In Genesis 3, Adam and Eve disobeyed God. They lived according to their own wills instead of God's will. This sin put a barrier between themselves and God, ruining the perfect relationship of trust and love they were intended to have. So, in the Genesis story, the couple was punished for their sin; Adam and Eve were expelled from the Garden of Eden.

The story of sin is the human story since our earliest times. We are affected by sin today, in what the theologians call "original sin." We are sinful in our origins as people. The image of God in which we were created has been cracked, broken, or destroyed. We have lost the relationship of trust and love with God we were intended to have. This sin is serious, and we need a savior for our sin. Wonderfully, as we will see, God provided this savior by sending Jesus Christ into the world to die for our sin and restore the relationship of love our sin has broken. As Moltmann put it, "This is the dilemma: that according to the biblical traditions we have to talk about human beings as God's image and as sinners at the same time."[11]

Our dilemma is that we are sinners, yet created by God. Our lives can have meaning and purpose when they are lived in accord with God's will and in the ways

God desires. The good news of the Christian gospel is that God has acted to forgive our sin and restore us to the relationship God intends, in Jesus Christ. As created by God, and as redeemed by Jesus Christ, our lives can reflect the image of God the creator. They can be the best lives possible when they are lived in harmony with the will of God our creator.

GOD THE PROVIDER

The recognition that our lives can have meaning and purpose is possible not only if God is the one who creates but also if God is the one who provides. This is usually called the doctrine of providence. As mentioned earlier, if God had only been the creator and then had walked away from the creation—not upholding what was created with divine power—then all things would collapse. The creation would not have the power to continue to exist. But the Christian view is that God has not turned away from creation. Rather, God is intimately involved with creation. God is preserving creation, cooperating with humans in creation, and guiding creation according to God's will toward God's ultimate purposes. The final end of all things is the kingdom of God, or the reign of God. But on our way to the kingdom, God is actively involved in creation and in human history. God is working out divine purposes in accord with God's divine will. While we cannot know God's plan in detail, we have faith to believe that God is at work in history and in human lives to move the creation along toward the ultimate establishment of the eternal reign of God. Jesus taught his disciples to pray in the Lord's Prayer, "Your kingdom come. Your will be done, on earth as it is in heaven" (Matt. 6:10). At the end, "The kingdom of the world has become the kingdom of our Lord and of his Messiah, and he will reign forever and ever" (Rev. 11:15). God's purposes will be fulfilled.

John Calvin defined providence this way: "Let my readers grasp that providence means not that by which God idly observes from heaven what takes place on earth, but that by which, as keeper of the keys, he governs all events. Thus it pertains no less to his hands than to his eyes."[12] This claim is very comprehensive, and many questions are associated with it. Calvin spoke of a "general providence" through which God oversees and rules in the world and a "special providence" in which God is intimately involved in the lives of people. Calvin wrote that "the universe is ruled by God, not only because he watches over the order of nature set by himself, but because he exercises especial care over each of his works."[13]

Classically, Reformed theologians have spoken of three aspects of providence, three dimensions to help us understand the work of God in providing for the creation God has established.[14]

Preservation (Lat. *conservatio*). God's preservation of the creation is God continuing to provide the divine energy that enables the creation to continue to exist. This supporting power of God is necessary for the life of the world and for human lives, for each of us. We sing about it in a hymn: "Eternal God, whose power upholds both flower and flaming star."[15]

We all depend on God for our existence and for our continuing existence. We realize we have no "sufficiency" in and of ourselves to create our lives or to continue to live our lives without God's ongoing power. We may not think about this often. We take it for granted that we will live, day after day, night after night. But in the end, our lives depend on God. They depend on God's continuing, preserving power. The doctrine of God's providence gives us the assurance and comfort that our lives are secure in God's providential care. This trust allowed the psalmist to say, "I lie down and sleep; I wake again, for the LORD sustains me" (Ps. 3:5).

Cooperation (Lat. *concursus*). A second part of God's providence is cooperation. The great God cooperates with lesser powers in the universe, which means that the great God cooperates with us as humans. God accomplishes God's purposes in this world not simply by a divine decree alone. God accomplishes God's purposes in this world by working along with the human beings God has created. The psalmist prayed, "O prosper the work of our hands!" (Ps. 90:17). God works with us and through us to do God's will.

Humans have a genuine life to live, with decisions to make. As we make our decisions, we are cooperating—in one way or another—with the continuing purposes of God in this world. Our decisions may be ones that are pleasing to God or ones that are not. But our decisions are ours to make. They matter in God's overall plan. You and I are not puppets on a string, manipulated in our lives by a great puppet master. Instead, we are people who can and will choose certain actions. As

Christians, our hope—and joy—is that we can cooperate with God's purposes and live in ways that further
God's work in the world.

Guidance (Lat. *gubernatio*). God's work in this world
and God's plan for this world constitute God's work
of governance or guidance. God creates the universe,
sustains it, and is at work within it to carry out God's
ultimate will or ends or purposes. God guides human
history and all entities within it to reach their final goal
or *telos*.

This is the road toward the coming reign of God,
the rule of Jesus Christ, when "every knee should
bend . . . and every tongue should confess that Jesus
Christ is Lord" (Phil. 2:10). God is in history to win.
God has the means to win, and God means to win,
as Ernest T. Campbell once put it. In the big picture
story of the universe, the world, and the human family, God is working out divine purposes in all creation.
We are not given to know what those purposes are in
detail. As the hymn puts it, "O God, in a mysterious
way great wonders You perform."[16] Calvin wrote that
God's "wonderful method of governing the universe
is rightly called an abyss, because while it is hidden
from us, we ought reverently to adore it."[17] But we are
assured that the coming reign of God that Jesus proclaimed and sought and was is taking shape now in the
historical moments of our world.

God is at work in the big picture of history. God is
also at work within the lives we lead. This is the comfort of the doctrine of providence. God is at work for
good purposes in our lives because God is good, God is
love, and God is working within us to establish God's

goodness and love for us. Calvin wrote that our knowledge of God's providence is "gratitude of mind for the favorable outcome of things, patience in adversity, and also incredible freedom from worry about the future."[18] God's providence brings comfort. Again, as Calvin wrote, we have a "never-failing assurance . . . from knowing that, when the world appears to be aimlessly tumbled about, the Lord is everywhere at work, and from trusting that his work will be for [our] welfare."[19]

We see God's providence best in retrospect, when we look back over our lives. Then we see the ways God has guided and worked within us and among us to carry out God's purposes. We have the same assurance for the future. God will continue to guide us. The challenge of providence is to seek and to find God's best will for us so that we can faithfully and joyfully carry out God's purposes. This is the great, personal benefit of the doctrine of providence. Calvin said that "if you pay attention, you will easily perceive that ignorance of providence is the ultimate of all miseries; the highest blessedness lies in the knowledge of it."[20]

THE GOD WHO CREATES AND GUIDES

The Bible tells us of a God who created the world. God created a good world. God created human beings within the world. Humans disobeyed God and have disrupted the relationship God desires between God and God's creation. Even the natural or physical world suffers from the effects of this sin. So the good creation has been spoiled. Only God can set things right again, which is what God has done in the person and work of Jesus Christ. We humans are dependent on God for our life itself and for any goodness that can emerge in our lives. The triune God—Father, Son, and Holy Spirit—is a God of love. We depend on God. We find our greatest purposes in life by recognizing our Creator God and seeking to serve God.

This Creator God is also the providing God. The God of providence is active in the world. God upholds the creation, continuing to sustain it by the divine power. God cooperates with us in our lives in the created order. We seek to know and do God's will. We trust God to lead us in the ways God wants. We trust God because we also believe that God governs or guides both the creation itself and human history, but also the individual lives we lead. The doctrine of providence is the great assurance to us that God will never leave us or forsake us. We can trust God to be at work to carry out divine purposes in our lives even when, at times, our way is dark or dangerous or when we are anxious or fearful. God will not let us down. God will not let us go. We have the assurance and comfort and joy we need for living. We also have the challenge of seeking God's will and doing it. Our creator and providing God has shown us the greatest love in sending Jesus Christ into the world to live and die and be raised again for our sakes. The creating and providing God has a human face: the face of our Lord and Savior, Jesus Christ.

Chapter 3

CONFESSING
JESUS CHRIST TODAY

CHRISTIANS GATHER ROUND JESUS CHRIST. JESUS OF
Nazareth, as he is known to us in the pages of the New
Testament, is the one we worship and serve, the one
who is like us and yet unlike us. He is the one to whom
the Bible looks and anticipates, the one whom we now
name as our Lord and Savior. Jesus Christ is central to
Christianity and to Christian faith. All who belong to
Christian churches confess their allegiance and obedience to Jesus Christ. He is the one whom we believe
in as the eternal Word of God (John 1:1), God's eternal Son. He is the one to whom, in the end, "at the
name of Jesus every knee should bend, in heaven and
on earth and under the earth, and every tongue should

confess that Jesus Christ is Lord, to the glory of God the Father" (Phil. 2:10–11).

WHERE WE HAVE BEEN

The Reformed tradition has always affirmed truths about Jesus Christ from the creeds of the ancient church. Our Reformed tradition has its roots in the theologies of Huldrych Zwingli and John Calvin in the sixteenth century, as well as other important theologians of that period, such as Heinrich Bullinger, Martin Bucer, and others. In addition, we honor creeds and confessions of the Reformation period. Our Reformed tradition has a rich confessional heritage that is available to us today as we seek to make a faithful confession of who Jesus Christ is and what Jesus Christ has done for salvation.

We have hosts of theologians, confessions, and sustained thought in the Reformed tradition on the matter of Jesus Christ—because Jesus Christ is so central to our Christian faith. Beyond the early days of the Reformed tradition we have even more. All major theologians must deal with Christology, their views of Jesus Christ. Reformed creeds and confessions in the previous centuries all address christological issues in some form. We have much from which to draw.

REFORMED CHRISTOLOGY

Core Christological Issues. As we draw on these sources, we find that Reformed thought agrees on the core christological issues. Our theologians, confessions, and christological writings pick up the essential insights from the early church as it confessed Jesus Christ as Lord and Savior and explored the implications of that confession. The early Reformed tradition and leaders such as Calvin and Zwingli affirmed and reaffirmed the primary insights and expressions of who Jesus Christ is, as understood by the early church in its creeds and also in the Chalcedonian formula of AD 451.

At the Council of Chalcedon, the church gave a definitive statement of who Jesus was in light of various heresies and theological proposals that had become popular. Chalcedon affirmed Jesus Christ as one person with two natures—a divine and human nature. He is "truly God and truly a human being." Chalcedon goes on to give those memorable descriptors that Jesus Christ is "acknowledged to be unconfusedly, unalterably, undividedly, inseparably in two natures." Jesus Christ is "coessential with the Father as to his deity and coessential with us—the very same one—as to his humanity." Our Reformed confessions say "amen" to this, with the Scots Confession picking up the concept in its chapter, "The Incarnation of Christ Jesus."[1]

So Jesus Christ is one person with two natures, divine and human. He is unique, the only person who ever lived of whom this can be said, which is why he is Lord and Savior. He has the power to save us, and he *has* saved us through his life, death, and resurrection. Jesus' uniqueness as a person—a real human person—enables him to be the one to bring salvation to the world. This is why Heinrich Bullinger's Second Helvetic Confession of 1566 says,

> Jesus Christ is the Only Savior of the World, and the
> True Awaited Messiah. For we teach and believe that
> this Jesus Christ our Lord is the unique and eternal Sav-
> ior of the human race, and thus of the whole world, in
> whom by faith are saved all who before the law, under
> the law, and under the Gospel were saved, and how-
> ever many will be saved at the end of the world.[2]

Then follow Scripture citations and the statement,
"God appointed him beforehand and sent him to us, so
that we are not now to look for any other." Bullinger's
confession was one of the most widely used Reformed
confessions of the sixteenth century. Jesus Christ is the
incarnate Son of God—truly God and truly human.
This is called the "hypostatic union" (*unio hypostasis*),
or the union of the "person." Jesus had two natures,
but they together constituted one person.

Reformed Christology doesn't stop there. In
Reformed thought, the purpose of the person of Christ
is for salvation. These formulations about who Jesus
Christ is are not just speculative theories that emerge
from ivory-tower theologians. No. Jesus Christ came
into the world to save sinners. It is "while we still were
sinners" that "Christ died for us" (Rom. 5:8). The Heidelberg Catechism captures this for us in two of its
questions and answers:

**Q. 29. Why is the Son of God called JESUS,
which means SAVIOR?**
A. Because he saves us from our sins, and because
salvation is to be sought or found in no other.

**Q. 30. Do those who seek their salvation and
well-being from saints, by their own efforts, or by
other means really believe in the only Savior Jesus?**

A. No. Rather, by such actions they deny Jesus, the only Savior and Redeemer, even though they boast of belonging to him. It therefore follows that either Jesus is not a perfect Savior, or those who receive this Savior with true faith must possess in him all that is necessary for their salvation.[3]

Put succinctly, as Reformed scholar Jan Rohls writes, "The incarnation of God's Son is the indispensable presupposition for the Son of God to carry out the work of reconciliation."[4] So, the person and the work of Christ go together in Reformed thought. God has become a human being in the man Jesus so that reconciliation, salvation, peace, and liberation of humans from their sins may happen.

Varieties of Expression. Another point to be made is that the Reformed confessions express their christological teachings about the person and work of Christ in a variety of ways, using a range of images and an assortment of expressions. In doing so, the confessions reflect the diversity of thought, images, and expressions we find within the Scriptures themselves in describing Jesus Christ and his work of redemption, salvation, and reconciliation.

This point could be expanded in a number of directions. But think of all the titles the Scriptures use to describe Jesus—terms such as Lord, Savior, Son of Man, Son of God, High Priest, Prophet, Door, Shepherd; the list goes on. All these are different ways to capture some aspect of who Jesus was.

Likewise with the work of Christ. The New Testament provides a number of biblical images for salvation. These images include reconciliation, liberation, expiation, redemption, and justification. In other words, salvation is reconciliation, it is liberation, it is expiation, and so on. Theologically we can see from the early church period that theologians thought of salvation in different ways, from various angles. For Justin Martyr, salvation was illumination—the enlightenment of the mind. For Irenaeus, salvation was restoration of the lost image of God. For Tertullian, it was satisfaction—an obedience that cancelled out inherited guilt. Origen presented a cosmic picture of "Christus victor"—Christ as victor over the powers of sin and evil. For Athanasius, salvation is deification, the divinization of humanity until we are ultimately united with God. For Augustine, salvation was expressed through the image of justification. We have this wide variety of images and these diverse theological ways of understanding the nature of salvation. In other words, we have a whole panorama of ways to express what Jesus Christ has done in his life, death, and resurrection.[5] This is to say nothing of the theories of the atonement that theologians have derived—their ways of explaining what the cross of Christ means and how the death of Jesus Christ has affected salvation for believers.[6]

The history of Christian thought—and Reformed theology, too—offers a wide range of ways of explaining what salvation is and how it has been accomplished in Jesus Christ. Unless a person denies the effectiveness of Jesus' death altogether, one cannot be a heretic on the doctrine of the atonement. Why? Because the Christian church (and Reformed theology) has never tried to limit the ways we understand the work of Christ. No one single formulation can do full justice to the biblical accounts and witness to who Jesus is and what Jesus has done.

Reformed theology reflects variations in its expressions, too. Besides the sixteenth-century documents we've cited, we move on in history to hear the Theological Declaration of Barmen (1934), which says that "Jesus Christ, as he is attested for us in Holy Scripture, is the one Word of God which we have to hear and which we have to trust and obey in life and in death."[7]

The Confession of 1967 startles us perhaps because it presents a "Christology from below," as the theologians say, which means its description of Jesus Christ does not begin from the divine side but from the human side. It does not begin with John 1:14 ("the Word became flesh and lived among us"). It begins from the man Jesus himself. The Confession says, "In Jesus of Nazareth, true humanity was realized once for all. Jesus, a Palestinian Jew, lived among his own people and shared their needs, temptations, joys, and sorrows. He expressed the love of God in word and deed and became a brother to all kinds of sinful men."[8] Beginning with the human nature of Jesus is just as valid theologically as beginning with the divine nature in describing who Jesus Christ is.

The Brief Statement of Faith of the Presbyterian Church (U.S.A.) (1991) emphasizes the life of Jesus as well as his death:

> We trust in Jesus Christ,
>   fully human, fully God.
> Jesus proclaimed the reign of God:
>   preaching good news to the poor
>   and release to the captives,

> teaching by word and deed
>   and blessing the children,
> healing the sick
>   and binding up the brokenhearted,
> eating with outcasts,
> forgiving sinners,
> and calling all to repent and believe the gospel.[9]

The Brief Statement of Faith goes on to say that "Jesus was crucified, suffering the depths of human pain and giving his life for the sins of the world." This christological approach or method is different.

So we have in our Reformed tradition these varieties of biblical and theological approaches and ways of understanding the person and work of Christ. The Confession of 1967 captures these different approaches as follows:

> God's reconciling act in Jesus Christ is a mystery which the Scriptures describe in various ways. It is called the sacrifice of a lamb, a shepherd's life given for his sheep, atonement by a priest; again it is ransom of a slave, payment of debt, vicarious satisfaction of a legal penalty, and victory over the powers of evil. These are expressions of a truth which remains beyond the reach of all theory in the depths of God's love for man. They reveal the gravity, cost, and sure achievement of God's reconciling work.[10]

The truth of who Jesus is and what Jesus has done is a truth that *does* remain beyond the reach of all theory.

CONFESSIONS AS HUMAN EXPRESSIONS

Reformed Christians understand all confessional statements and indeed all theological statements as human ways of trying to express God's ultimate truth that is over and beyond what any human words or theological theories can capture. Our confessional as well as our other theological statements are human attempts to say as much as we can express, as well as we can. But we realize at the same time that all our language is limited, all our theological statements are limited, and all our doctrinal formulations are open for revision if we find better ways of expressing what we believe the Scriptures teach us.[11] We Presbyterian and Reformed Christians base our confessions of faith on the Scriptures. We want them to be grounded in biblical truths. We are "reformed and always being reformed according to God's Word," as an old saying puts it. But the way we express our confessions or theology or doctrinal statements—these expressions are necessarily limited, time-bound, and open to revision. What we say is true; our statements confessionally and theologically are the best expressions we can construct. But none of them can do full justice to the whole witness of Scripture. Due to human limitations, and even sinfulness, all our theological and confessional statements are simply attempts to be true to what we hear God saying to us in the words of Scripture.

These things especially pertain to Christology. Our Reformed heritage affirms the historic, ortho-dox teachings of the early church. All our confessions attest to this. But they all attest to Jesus Christ in their own distinctive ways, formulating their descriptions in different fashions. Why? Simply because for all theology—and especially for Christology, which is so central, so key, so rich in its fullness—no one way of describing who Jesus is and what he has done can do justice to the whole range of what the Scriptures have to say about Christ's person and work. I like the statement said to be from a liberal theologian of the last century, Shailer Matthews of the University of Chicago. Matthews said that the reason there was darkness over the face of the earth from the sixth hour to the ninth hour when Jesus was being crucified was so that "no one could go home and say they had seen it all." We can never see *all* of what God has done in the person and work of Jesus Christ. We Presbyterians recognize this truth. We try to express as clearly and biblically as possible what we know. But we are always open to new dimensions, new insights, and new winds of God's Spirit that can lead us to new truths and to confess Jesus Christ in new terms.[12] If this were not so, our theology would be static and untouched by God's ongoing work in the world and in the church through the Spirit. So we affirm the diversities as well as the historic ways in which Christology is expressed in our Reformed tradition.

WHAT CAN WE SAY?

In light of the past and present convictions of the Reformed tradition, what can we say about confessing Jesus Christ today? Where has all our past and our present left us? What issues are key for us? How does all this look in the perspective of the Reformed family?

In relation to Reformed Christology, we all, as Reformed Christians, should be able to agree on some elements in light of what we've seen, our tradition, and our theological understandings.

BACKGROUND PERSPECTIVES

Reformed Christology Is Orthodox. In terms of background, let us be clear that our Reformed Christology, as found particularly in our confessional statements, is absolutely, thoroughly orthodox. We stand in direct continuity with the creeds and confessions of the early church, including the formula of Chalcedon, in affirming Jesus Christ as a member of the Holy Trinity, the eternal Son of God, who shares the divine essence and has become incarnate—has become a person—with two natures, divine and human. Jesus Christ is "truly God and truly human." On this our confessional heritage is clear.

Varieties of Christological Expressions Exist. Also, in terms of background, we can recognize that varieties of christological expressions exist within our confessions—as they do within the Scriptures themselves. What does this mean for us? One thing is that we have a great freedom of expression, a great panorama of images through which we can proclaim Jesus Christ. We are free to explore new images while maintaining the essential insights of the historic theological tradition. But in conjunction with this, we also realize that the varieties of christological expressions should warn us against absolutizing any one image, expression, or form of language in saying who Jesus Christ is and what he has done. If we insist on only one way or only one set of words by which Jesus Christ can be proclaimed and confessed, we're in danger of truncating the biblical witness and certainly not being consistent with our theological heritage. Jesus Christ has many faces, and what he has done in his life, death, and resurrection is expressed in a multitude of terms—some very simple, some quite complex.

Our varieties of christological expression biblically and historically open for us new ways of speaking theologically of Jesus in the present time

Jesus Christ Is the Unique Savior. A third background thought is that the christological statements of the Reformed tradition do not allow us to assert as an article of belief that there are paths or ways to God other than through Jesus Christ. We have no explicit biblical or confessional basis to make this proclamation as a statement of fact, or even faith. Jesus Christ as he is portrayed in the New Testament and in our Reformed confessions is the one Mediator between God and humanity, the unique and only Savior who has the power to save us from our sin because of who he was: truly divine and truly human. We know of no other saviors. To assert that such other saviors have lived goes beyond the limits and is contrary to Reformed Christology.

THEOLOGICAL CONVICTIONS

On the matter of salvation, we need to say three important things about the issue of Jesus Christ as Lord and what that means in regard to salvation. These things will help us as we confess Jesus Christ today.[13]

1. *The Freedom of God Is Paramount.* One of the great central convictions of Reformed theology is that God is

free. Another way to put it is, "God is sovereign." That is, God acts according to the divine will and is perfectly free to do whatever God chooses or purposes. God's actions are in accord with God's person—God's being and doing are one. This is why the Reformed have so strongly stressed the doctrine of election or predestination. God is perfectly free—to be God. God is perfectly free to save whomever God wants to save. God owes no one. Further, as we saw from the Second Helvetic Confession, God is free to save persons *through whatever means God chooses to use.* This confession indicated that while the normal means for salvation is through the preaching of the Word, "At the same time we recognize that God can illuminate whom and when he will, even without the external ministry, for that is in his power."[14] God can save us by whatever means God chooses—why? —simply because God is free. To say otherwise, or to say that some other external force or power (or theory!) can tell God what God *must* do— that is surely to create *another God.* So God is sovereign. God is free.

What is the implication of this? One is that if we wish to honor this theological principle that is so basic to Reformed thought, we will recognize that no humans—not even pious Christians—can prescribe to God who God may or must or should save. We as Christians cannot limit God's freedom or even assert that we know how God *must act* in regard to human salvation. God is free—free to save or not, according to the divine will.

This theological recognition of the freedom of God was particularly important to the Reformed theologian

Karl Barth. Barth's theology moved in the direction of universalism. Universalism is the view that all people will be saved by God. It has been around in Christian theology from the days of the early church (though never as the majority viewpoint). The early church theologian Origen taught it. Universalism means that all people—regardless of who they are or how evil we think they are—will be saved.

But Barth pulled back from making this ultimate leap into universalism, precisely because of the theological principle of the freedom of God. God is free. Barth wrote,

> If we are to respect the freedom of divine grace, we cannot venture the statement that it must and will finally be coincident with the world of [humans] as such (as in the doctrine of the so-called *apokatastasis* [universalism]). No such right or necessity can legitimately be deduced. Just as the gracious God does not need to elect or call any single [person], so [God] does not need to elect or call all [hu]mankind.[15]

Barth would not posit universalism because, as Donald Bloesch put it, "This would tie the grace of God to a law or principle and thereby compromise his sovereign freedom."[16]

The freedom of God allows God to choose whom to elect (in the traditional doctrine of election). But this freedom of God also keeps us from telling God, "God—you are love, you are gracious, therefore, you *must* save the whole world through universalism." In truth, whether God saves only Christians or only "religious" people or all people—that is God's free decision. Just as Barth argued that universalism as a principle limits God's freedom, so also do restrictive views that dictate how God must act.

So whatever we ultimately say about Jesus Christ—who he is and what he has done—we have to recognize that these are our statements of faith, our convictions of what God has or will do in Christ. We can in no way bind God to act or do something just because we believe we know correctly what God "should" do, even when we think we are rightly interpreting the Bible. Imagine our embarrassment in heaven if we get there and find that all the earth's people are there and that no one is excluded. Will we have the courage to tell God that God has acted wrongly? God's freedom is paramount.

2. *Christians Confess and Radically Proclaim Jesus Christ as Lord and Savior.* The Christian mandate is to "be my witnesses" (Acts 1:8), to proclaim the gospel, and to announce the "good news of great joy" to all people (Luke 2:10). This is the "go" in "gospel"; we go into all the world to preach the gospel (Matt. 28:20). The gospel we proclaim is the gospel message of Jesus Christ, our Lord and Savior. He is "the way, and the truth, and the life" (John 14:6). He is the "image of the invisible God, the firstborn of all creation" (Col. 1:15; cf. 1:19–20). For God was "in Christ . . . reconciling the world" (2 Cor. 5:19). This is the evangelical impulse for preaching and teaching for the church throughout the world.

Recognizing God's freedom to act and God's revelation in Jesus Christ should enhance the vigor with which the church today confesses and radically proclaims Jesus Christ as Lord and Savior. Salvation as we know it comes by God's revelation in Jesus Christ.

We can proclaim Jesus Christ with all the passion and power possible because we do genuinely believe that through him salvation is extended to the world. The Presbyterian Christian never apologizes for this faith commitment. Our confessional statements proclaim Jesus Christ and "lift high the cross" as the means God uses to bring reconciliation, liberation, peace, and all the rest of the images—in short, salvation. So we are "evangelicals"—entrusted with the *evangel*, the good news. We proclaim that gospel with all our might and energy because it is centered in our Lord and Savior, Jesus Christ.

3. *The Holy Spirit Is at Work More Widely Than We Can Know.* This is a theological given. We never know where or when or how the Spirit of God is or will be at work in our world and among people. We all have many personal experiences that can attest to this. The Spirit, says Jesus in the Gospel of John, "blows where it chooses" (3:8). We cannot prescribe the Spirit's comings and goings. We cannot know or understand the Spirit's ways. The freedom of the Spirit is as much a Reformed conviction as any other (especially in light of the Reformed tradition's emphases on election and predestination).

Might the Spirit of God be at work for salvation in other faiths? Perhaps. We honestly do not know. Is the Spirit of God at work in ways more widely than we can know? Yes—assuredly. We cannot prescribe or limit the Spirit's work in terms of salvation. If this is true, then we should at least be modest and humble and honest enough to say that *how* God chooses to save people—whatever people—by and through the work of the Spirit (which is the only way we know of by which people are saved) is, again, ultimately God's decision. God is free. The Spirit is free. We can never proclaim that we know when or where or how God's Spirit will be at work or efficacious for salvation. Calvin spoke of God's "secret work" of the Spirit. Through this work, the Spirit can affect and effect whatever God desires. We cannot prescriptively close the door to the wider work of the Holy Spirit. Rather, we should celebrate it!

CONFESSING JESUS CHRIST TODAY

In short, we do not know the limits of God's grace. The old hymn says, "There's a Wideness in God's Mercy."[17] Are there any limits to the grace of God?

We must pray for the salvation of those who may never come to know Christ. We pray for them each and every day. We pray for the church's mission and ministry in proclaiming Jesus Christ in both word and deed.

Then we also know that for us the assurance of salvation is found only in confessing Christ and trusting him alone. The memorable words of the first question of the Heidelberg Catechism ring in our ears: "What is your only comfort, in life and in death? Answer: 'That I belong—body and soul, in life and in death—not to myself but to my faithful Savior, Jesus Christ.' "[18]

Reformed Christians have squabbled much and wrestled mightily over theology for centuries. To us, as Presbyterian Christians, theology matters! We continue today in the wake of the early Reformers. We honor Jesus Christ our Lord in the words of the Second Helvetic Confession as "the unique and eternal Savior of

the human race, and thus of the whole world."[19] Our
theological statements should be made in all humility,
recognizing our limits as fallible and sinful interpreters
of Holy Scripture. We can and must have the courage
of our convictions. We have many convictions about
Jesus Christ. But we also must work together with our
brothers and sisters in Christ to proclaim and honor
our "one Lord, one faith." In our christological discus-
sions, debates, and deliberations, may we "[speak] the
truth in love" (Eph. 4:15) while we seek the unity of
the body of Christ that is marked by "bearing with one
another in love, making every effort to maintain the
unity of the Spirit in the bond of peace" (Eph. 4:2–3).
Let us remember the words from the book of Jude:
"Beloved, build yourselves up on your most holy faith;
pray in the Holy Spirit; keep yourselves in the love
of God; look forward to the mercy of our Lord Jesus
Christ that leads to eternal life" (Jude 20–21).

Chapter 4

THE HOLY SPIRIT
IN CHURCH AND WORLD

SOME YEARS AGO, A BOOK APPEARED TITLED *THE HOLY Spirit: Shy Member of the Trinity.*[1] This is perhaps who the Holy Spirit is for many of us. We are used to thinking about God the Father, God the Son, but God the Holy Spirit—not so much, or not so often! The Holy Spirit is the member of the Trinity who seems to be the most unknown. The Spirit sounds mysterious. The Spirit is elusive—we do not know much about what the Spirit does or how we should regard the Holy Spirit. The main members of the Trinity often seem to be God the creator and Jesus Christ the redeemer. What do we know of the Holy Spirit who is, like the other two members of the Godhead, also at work in the church and in the world?[2]

THE SPIRIT IS GOD WITH US

One of the important issues faced by the early church was how to understand the Holy Spirit. The "Spirit of God" was a phrase often used in the Hebrew Scriptures. The Hebrew term *ruach* means "breath" or "wind" and also "spirit." Biblical images for the Spirit include

- "life-breath," as when the "breath" of God brings life to human beings (Gen. 2:7);
- "wind," as when Jesus says the "Spirit" of God is like the wind that blows where it chooses when Jesus was telling Nicodemus about the new birth (John 3:3–8);
- "fire," as when John the Baptist preached about the Coming One who would baptize with the Spirit and with fire (Matt. 3:11); and
- "water," as when salvation comes as "water on the thirsty land, and streams on the dry ground" in the book of Isaiah (44:3), or when Jesus used "water" as a symbol for God's Spirit (John 4:10; 7:38–39).

These different images give vitality, an energy to the Spirit. They show God's Spirit at work in the world. God's Spirit makes a difference in the here and now. God's Spirit is God with us, wherever we may be.

This recognition of God's Spirit at work, described further in both the Hebrew Scriptures and the New Testament, led early Christians to eventually recognize the Spirit of God as equal to the Son of God and to God the Father as the three members of the Trinity. The

Holy Spirit shared the same substance as the Father and the Son. The Spirit shares the same nature as the Son and the Father. Yet this recognition did not happen overnight. Some theologians perceived the Holy Spirit as a bit less than God the Father and God the Son. The Spirit was a lesser God—not fully equal or sharing the same divinity as the Father and the Son. But largely through the efforts of theologians from the Eastern church (the Cappadocians), the Christian church came to the view that Father, Son, and Holy Spirit are three persons who are one God. Each of the three members of the Trinity is fully and equally "God." In the Nicene Creed of AD 381, the church confessed in the original version, "We believe in the Holy Spirit, the Lord, the Giver of Life, who proceeds from the Father, who with the Father and the Son is worshiped and glorified."[3] The Christian church accepted the full equality of the Holy Spirit as God with the Son and the Father. The church confessed the Holy Spirit as God with us.

THE SPIRIT AND THE CHURCH

Christians believe that the Holy Spirit of God is active in the church and in the world. Our Reformed theological tradition has had a very robust view of the work of the Holy Spirit, in the work of theologians and in confessional documents. The work of the Spirit is key in areas such as the authority of Scripture, coming to faith in Jesus Christ, one's growth in the Christian life, and the mission of the church in the world, along with many other topics. Throughout, of course, since the Holy Spirit is a member of the Trinity, all the activities of the Spirit are the work of God. God is with us in the church and the world by the Spirit.

To see this more clearly, consider some of the important dimensions of the work of the Holy Spirit— first, in the church.

Scripture and Spirit. The Reformed have always emphasized that it is by the work of the Holy Spirit that we come to believe the Bible is the Word of God. John Calvin said, "Without the illumination of the Holy Spirit, the Word can do nothing."[4] It is not by reason or arguments but by the "internal witness (testimony) of the Holy Spirit" through which God acts to bring us to the conviction—or faith—that Scripture is God's Word. We acknowledge Scripture as God's Word when we recognize, as Calvin said, that "God in person speaks in it."[5] This conviction comes, Calvin said, when we seek "a higher place than human reasons, judgments, or conjectures, that is, in the secret testimony of the Spirit."[6] This testimony, he claimed, is "more excellent than all reason."[7] For those whom the Holy Spirit has illuminated in this way, Scripture becomes "self-authenticated" as the Spirit "seals" the Scripture in our hearts. This presence of the Spirit provides a personal certainty that Scripture "has flowed to us from the very mouth of God by the ministry of men."[8] So the "internal witness" of the Holy Spirit enables us to come to believe that Scripture is the Word of God, God's own self-revelation that has authority for our lives.

Spirit and Sin. Relatedly, the work of the Holy Spirit convinces us or convicts us of our sin. Sin is our separation from God, our alienation from our creator who loves us. Sin is our seeking our own ways in life, without regard or concern for whom God wants us to be or what God wants us to do. This sin separates us from God and from God's purposes for us. It also leads, eventually, to our eternal separation from God. As Paul wrote to the Romans, "For the wages of sin is death" (Rom. 6:23). We need a remedy for our sin. We need a way for our sin to be forgiven. We need good news in the midst of the bad news all around us—and within us.

The good news that God provides is the gospel of Jesus Christ. Jesus Christ came to live and die and be raised again from the dead so that our sin may be forgiven, so that our alienation from God can be overcome. This is the story of salvation. It is the message of "good news of great joy for all the people" (Luke 2:10). In the death and resurrection of Jesus Christ our relationship with God can be restored. The separation that sin brought has been overcome by the reconciliation God provides in Jesus Christ. This is the gospel.

We know this gospel message through the power and work of the Holy Spirit. The Spirit shows us that we are sinners. The Spirit reveals our sin and then gives us the greatest gift of all: the gift of faith in Jesus Christ, our Savior and Lord.

Spirit and Faith. The Holy Spirit establishes faith in Jesus Christ within us and joins us with Christ in the bond of faith. Through the "secret energy of the Spirit, we come to enjoy Christ and all his benefits,"[9] said Calvin. The "testimony of the Spirit" is a "testimony we feel engraved like a seal upon our hearts, with the result that it seals the cleansing and sacrifice of Christ." Calvin said that "we cannot come to Christ unless we be drawn by the Spirit of God."[10] The Holy Spirit is "the bond by which Christ unites us to himself." So the Spirit is the means by which Christian believers live in Christ and are united with Christ in their growth in faith. Calvin indicates the Holy Spirit is called "the 'Spirit of sanctification' [cf. II Thess. 2:13; 1 Peter 1:2; Rom. 1:4] because he not only quickens and nourishes us by a general power that is visible both in the human race and in the rest of the living creatures, but he is also the root and seed of heavenly life in us."[11] The Spirit enables our faith in Christ to develop and be expressed in love (Gal. 5:6).

Faith, Calvin maintains, is "the principal work of the Holy Spirit."[12] Faith in Jesus Christ is "sealed" in our hearts by the Holy Spirit, who is "the inner teacher," said Calvin, "by whose effort the promise of salvation penetrates into our minds, a promise that would otherwise only strike the air or beat upon our ears." In short, "Faith itself has no other source than the Spirit." The great importance of this work of the Holy Spirit in establishing faith in the heart is such that the Spirit "may rightly be called the key that unlocks for us the treasures of the Kingdom of Heaven [cf. Rev. 3:7]." As William Placher put it, "The doctrine of the Holy Spirit affirms that not only the Word through whom God is revealed to us, but the Spirit through whom we come to believe, is God."[13]

These aspects of the work of the Holy Spirit are crucial for Christian theology and for Christian life, according to our Reformed tradition. Spirit and Word are inextricably bound up together. Spirit and faith are intimately joined. But notice that in both these cases, the work of the Holy Spirit is not to call attention to the Spirit. The work of the Spirit is to witness or bear testimony to Jesus Christ. The Spirit bears witness to Scripture as God's Word in which we are presented with Jesus Christ. The Spirit establishes faith, which is faith directed to the person of Jesus Christ as the eternal Son of God, our Lord and Savior. The Spirit always points beyond. The Spirit points beyond the Spirit to point to Jesus Christ. The great theologian Karl Barth put it simply when he said that "the only content of the Holy Spirit is Jesus."[14] "There is no special or second revelation of the Spirit alongside that of the Son," said Barth.[15] The Spirit and the Word collaborate together, along with the Father, to bring the miracle of faith in a human heart.

Some Christian traditions emphasize the Holy Spirit.[16] They focus on outward, visible displays of the Spirit such as speaking in tongues. One must "have the Spirit" or be "slain in the Spirit" to be recognized as a true Christian believer in these traditions. But the Reformed have seen the Holy Spirit at work, not in the outward, dramatic displays that emphasize the visible expressions of the Spirit that call attention to the Spirit, but as the One who witnesses to Jesus Christ. The Spirit is that "shy member of the Trinity" who in the New Testament does not call attention to the Spirit, but who is at work in miraculous ways to bring us to the conviction that Scripture is the Word of God and that Jesus Christ is the Son of God. So the work of the Holy Spirit in the church is vitally important in our Reformed faith. Without the Spirit, there would be no Scripture and no Christian faith.

Spirit Calls the Church. If the principal work of the Holy Spirit is faith, as Calvin said, then it is the Holy Spirit who calls forth the church. The apostle Paul said, "No one can say 'Jesus is Lord' except by the Holy Spirit" (1 Cor. 12:3). It is the internal witness of the Holy Spirit that enables us to confess Jesus Christ as our Lord and Savior as the Spirit grants faith so that we become members of the church of Jesus Christ. Faith is the mark of the Christian. Faith is the gift of the Holy Spirit. Faith unites us to Jesus Christ. Faith is the bond of the disciples of Jesus Christ with Christ and with one another in the Christian church. As Calvin wrote, "Christ, when he illumines us into faith by the power of his Spirit, at the same time so engrafts us into his body that we become partakers of every good."[17]

Calvin reminds us that faith is the gift of the grace of God and also that it is God through the Spirit who initiates faith. Faith is not our own, human achievement. It is the gift of God. As Paul said, "By grace you have been saved through faith, and this is not your own doing; it is the gift of God—not the result of works, so that no one may boast" (Eph. 2:8–9). The Holy Spirit calls the church together as the people of faith. The Spirit is "prior" to the church. The Holy Spirit initiates the church by the grace and calling of God.[18]

This is a basic Reformed theological emphasis. In all things, the initiative to begin is with God. God is the one who wills, decides, elects, calls, and brings to pass what happens. God chooses to give the gift of faith by the work of the Holy Spirit. The Roman Catholic theologian Hans Küng caught hold of this insight when he wrote, "The Spirit of God comes first; and through the Spirit God in his freedom *creates* the Church, and constantly creates it anew from those who believe." He continued, "But the believers who congregate in the Church do not summon themselves. They do not even summon themselves to faith. God himself calls them through the word of Christ in the power of the Holy Spirit to faith and hence to the Church as the fellowship of the faithful. God in the Holy Spirit acts in perfect freedom."[19]

Küng has described the essential New Testament insight, which also became a Reformed insight, that God is free and that the Spirit precedes the church, calling and gathering the church together through the gift of faith in Jesus Christ.

Spirit and Election. When Küng described the church as the "fellowship of the faithful," he could have said, "the company of the elect." In Reformed thought, the true church is the "elect of God," those whom God has chosen to receive the gift of faith in Jesus Christ by the work of the Holy Spirit (see Eph. 1:3–14).[20] Election is another way of saying "salvation by grace." Calvin wrote, "Rare indeed is the mind that is not repeatedly struck with this thought: whence comes your salvation but from God's election?"[21] Our faith in Jesus Christ is God's work within us by the Holy Spirit. Our faith does not depend on our own abilities, merits, or works. Our whole salvation rests in the work of God. We receive this salvation—which is totally by God's grace—through the gift of faith, which is the work of the Holy Spirit. Calvin called this "the inestimable fruit of comfort" that election brings.[22] The Holy Spirit gives us faith, which is the bond that unites us to Jesus Christ, through whom God has provided for our salvation by the divine, eternal election.

Spirit and Regeneration. The Holy Spirit gives us the gift of faith as a sign of our election. What happens in us, in our lives, when we receive the gift of faith in Jesus Christ is called regeneration. Calvin wrote, "Whomsoever God wills to snatch from death, he quickens by the Spirit of regeneration."[23] Regeneration means "rebirth" or "new birth" (see John 3:3). It means being "born again" or becoming a "new creation." As Paul wrote to the Corinthians, "So if anyone is in Christ, there is a new creation: everything old has passed away; see, everything has become new!" (2 Cor. 5:17). Calvin said regeneration is "the beginning of the spiritual life."[24]

When we receive the gift of faith—to believe in Jesus Christ as our Lord and Savior, by the work of the Holy Spirit—our lives are made new. The power of sin within us is broken. Our minds, our hearts, our wills— our whole selves become a "new creation." We have a new nature. We are no longer people who are in sin; we are in Christ (see Gal. 2:20). Regeneration is our whole lives being made new in Jesus Christ by the power of the Holy Spirit.[25]

Spirit and Sanctification. The Holy Spirit begins our Christian life by confirming our election through the gift of faith, calling us into the church as the body of believers in Jesus Christ, and initiating our Christian life by making us "new creations" in Christ Jesus. Then our Christian life in the church is under way. We live our lives now as disciples of Jesus Christ, as the people of God, and we do so as the Holy Spirit of God leads us and guides us and works within and among us. This is what we call "sanctification." Sanctification means our growth in holiness, our growth in faith. Sanctification means our moving along in our Christian lives in the church to serve God more fully, to serve Christ more fully, and to become the people God intends and wants us to be. Sanctification is our Christian life. As Calvin put it, "For the Spirit is not only the initiator of faith, but increases it by degrees, until by it he leads us to the Kingdom of Heaven."[26] As 2 Timothy 1:14 says, "Guard the good treasure entrusted to you, with the help of the Holy Spirit living in us." The Holy Spirit is the member of the divine Trinity who works with the church and who dwells in the lives of Christian believers to lead us in the ways God wants us to live. As Karl Barth wrote, "The Holy Spirit is the living Lord Jesus Christ Himself in the work of the sanctification of His particular people in the world, of His community and all its members."[27]

The Holy Spirit shows us the directions we should go in the Christian life. Barth also saw that our sanctification as "the work of the Holy Spirit has to be described as the giving and receiving of direction. It is in this way that the Holy One creates the saints." Our "new form of existence" as Christian people, said Barth, is as "the true covenant-partner of God."[28] We follow God's will and God's way, in fellowship with God and by the power of the Spirit.

The Holy Spirit works within the Christian community, the church, and within the lives of Christian believers. The Spirit brings the gifts of faith and hope and love to the church. The Spirit guides the community and the Christian. The Spirit upholds the church

and Christian believers. The Spirit shows the order or
the form the church should take in regulating its life
and carrying out its mission. The Spirit directs our lives
as Christian believers toward the ways and purposes of
God for us in both the great and the small parts of our
lives. This is the doctrine of God's providence. God
leads us in the ways God would have us go by the work
of the Holy Spirit within our lives.

Spirit and Sacraments. The Holy Spirit also works in
relation to the sacraments of the church. The sacraments are one of God's ways of nurturing our faith.
A sacrament is often defined as an "outward sign of
an inward grace," a visible expression of an invisible
reality. Sacraments are God's way of reaching out to
us to give us ways of recognizing the reality of what
God has done. They refer us back to the Word of God
in Scripture and also make the Scriptures come alive
for us in important ways. Sacraments express and convey spiritual realities. They strengthen and nourish our
faith. They support and enable us in our Christian lives
and ministries. Sacraments strengthen the church in its
corporate faith.

The Holy Spirit gives the sacraments their effects.
Without the Spirit, sacraments are outward forms, ritu-
als without a direct power for those who participate in
them. Sacraments point to the mystery of God at work
among us. The Holy Spirit makes the message of God's
work real and energizing in our lives. The Spirit brings
efficacy or effectiveness to the work of God as we find
it in Holy Scripture, also bringing the effects of God's
work into our lives with power and meaning.

The two sacraments recognized in Reformed and Presbyterian churches are baptism and the Lord's Supper. In baptism, we are brought into or incorporated into the family of faith, the church. Baptism is an outward expression of our adoption into the family of God, showing we are all children of God's grace.[29] Reformed churches practice infant baptism as one form of the sacrament of baptism. The promises of God's love, expressed in the covenants of the Bible and supremely in the new covenant in Jesus Christ himself, are extended to us and to our children. We receive the benefits of God's election and love for us through the gospel of Jesus Christ. We express our acceptance of this grace of God by being baptized in the church and bringing our children to be baptized as infants so that the world will know that we belong to God in Christ and so that we will receive the benefits of God's love through faith. Augustine called a sacrament a "visible word." It represents, as Calvin put it, "God's promises as painted in a picture and sets them before our sight, portrayed graphically and in the manner of images."[30] The water of baptism is an outward expression of the inward cleansing of our sin and our reception into the household of faith. Right before our eyes, both in adult and in infant baptism, we see the water to remind us and to bring to us this forgiving power of God and this incorporation into the church of God. Calvin said that "baptism is the sign of the initiation by which we are received into the society of the church, in order that, engrafted in Christ, we may be reckoned among God's children."[31]

In the church, our faith is nourished by the Lord's Supper. Sacraments are signs and seals of God's promises to us. In the Lord's Supper—as we remember the Last Supper when Jesus broke the bread and poured the wine, anticipating his death—we receive the benefits of what Jesus Christ has done as a sign and a seal. The bread and the wine are the outward signs of the body and blood of Christ. As we participate in the Lord's Supper by faith, eating the bread and drinking the wine, the truth and reality and power of Christ's death are sealed within us by the power of the Holy Spirit. Calvin said the Lord's Supper is "a spiritual banquet, wherein Christ attests himself to be the life-giving bread, upon which our souls feed unto true and blessed immortality [John 6:54]."[32] In the Supper, "Refreshed by partaking of him, we may repeatedly gather strength until we shall have reached heavenly immortality." The Lord's Supper continually strengthens our faith and feeds our faith "as often as we eat and drink."

All this is possible only by the work of the Holy Spirit. Again, Calvin noted that "the sacraments properly fulfill their office only when the Spirit, that inward teacher, comes to them, by whose power alone hearts are penetrated and affections moved and our souls opened for the sacraments to enter in. If the Spirit be lacking, the sacraments can accomplish nothing more in our minds than the splendor of the sun shining upon blind eyes, or a voice sounding in deaf ears."[33] So the Holy Spirit is the energizer of the sacraments. The Spirit joined with the Word of God makes the sacraments a means of grace for us in the church and in the Christian life. Without the Spirit, sacraments are lifeless and dead. But by the power of the Spirit the sacraments are powerful expressions of the realities of God's acts of love, justice, and peace. They bring us into the household of faith and continually nourish and nurture our faith as we celebrate the sacraments in the church. Word and Spirit are bound together. The Spirit confirms and increases our faith through the sacraments.

THE SPIRIT AND THE WORLD

We are accustomed to looking for the work of the Holy Spirit in the church. The Holy Spirit of God is active in many ways we recognize in the ongoing life of the Christian church. But the Spirit is not limited to the church alone. The Spirit is active in the world. The Spirit is active in the world in ways beyond our knowing, in ways that are significant in the overall purposes and providence of God.

Lord and Giver of Life. In the Nicene Creed, from the early church, we confess our faith in the Holy Spirit, "the Lord and giver of life." The Spirit in Scripture is God's creative Spirit who brings life. This Spirit is at work in the world, beyond the church. The Reformed theologian Jürgen Moltmann wrote, "If Christ is confessed as the reconciler and head of the whole cosmos, as he is in the Epistle to the Colossians, then the Spirit is present wherever Christ is present, and has to be understood as the divine energy of life animating the new creation of all things."[34]

For Moltmann this means we who believe in the Spirit of God should be brought to a "new vitality of a

love for life." The Spirit of God is at work in the whole
cosmos, in the whole creation. All things in creation
gain their being and reality—their life—from the creative breath or spirit of God. Concerns today for the
earth as our environment, for ecology and the preservation of the creation are ways we live out the Spirit
of God as the creative, life-giving Spirit who brings
energy and vitality to all things. As Moltmann writes,
"To experience the fellowship of the Spirit inevitably
carries Christianity beyond itself into the greater fellowship of all God's creatures."[35] According to Moltmann, the church has to come into "solidarity with
the cosmos" to work for the preservation of the earth
and its creatures in the midst of the mortal threats that
are around us and that can bring "the annihilation of
God's earthly creation." Moltmann says that "discovery of the cosmic breadth of God's Spirit leads . . . to
respect for the dignity of all created things, in which
God is present through his Spirit. In the present situation this discovery is not romantic poetry or speculative vision. It is the essential premise for the survival of
humanity on God's one, unique earth."[36]

The Power of the Spirit. The Holy Spirit of God as
"the Lord and Giver of Life" gives power for our lives
to those of us who are united with Jesus Christ by faith
and sealed as the children of God. The Spirit brings
power to the church, but it is the power to carry out
God's will. The Spirit does not bring us power to exercise lordship over others. The Spirit of God is the Spirit
of love and justice. The Spirit communicates God's
own character to us, the character and reality of God
we see in the person of Jesus Christ. The Spirit brings

power to the church and to the Christian to live out a faithful discipleship in following Jesus Christ and seeking to do God's will in our corporate and personal lives.

In the Brief Statement of Faith of the Presbyterian Church (U.S.A.), the third part of the confession is, "We trust in God the Holy Spirit." Part of that affirmation reads:

> We trust in God the Holy Spirit,
>   everywhere the giver and renewer of life. . . .
> The Spirit gives us courage
>   to pray without ceasing,
>   to witness among all peoples to Christ as Lord and
>   Savior,
>   to unmask idolatries in Church and culture,
>   to hear the voices of peoples long silenced,
>   and to work with others for justice, freedom, and
>   peace.[37]

Here we see that the Spirit is active with the church and with Christian believers to work in the world spreading and sharing Jesus Christ as Lord and Savior. We call this "evangelism," the communication of the Christian gospel in word and deed. The Spirit gives power for sharing the message of Jesus Christ.

But we see that the Spirit is also active in the world in calling the church to name and "unmask" all those things that hinder the Spirit of God as the Spirit of life. These are idolatries that sinfully lead people away from the worship and service of the true God. By the power of the Spirit we seek to "unmask idolatries in Church and culture."

We see that the Spirit of God gives power "to hear the voices of peoples long silenced." The quest for human freedom and liberation is a quest that is enabled by the Spirit of God and a quest in which the church of Jesus Christ can share. The Spirit brings power for new life and freedom.

We see that the Spirit of God gives power for the church to "work with others for justice, freedom, and peace." These are values the Spirit works to establish in the world. Justice, freedom, and peace are fruits of the Spirit of God as they bring life and new life, insofar as they renew the lives of people in great need and people who cry out for the Spirit of God in their lives and their societies.

The Spirit brings life and the Spirit brings power for us to seek new life in the Spirit for ourselves, for our churches, and for the world.

THE SPIRIT AT WORK IN CHURCH AND WORLD

While the Holy Spirit may be the "shy member of the Trinity," the Spirit is certainly an active member of the Trinity. The Spirit is God with us, at work in more ways than we can possibly know or realize. The Spirit works in the church, spreading gifts among Christian believers—the gifts of faith, hope, and love. The Spirit is at work in the world, as the Lord and Giver of life whose power is at work in and throughout the whole cosmos. The Spirit is working in the lives of people who are unaware of the Spirit's reality or presence.

We should be deeply grateful for the work of the Holy Spirit. On the Spirit we depend for every breath we take, for the gift of life itself. The Spirit brings knowledge of our sin and then knowledge of the deepest reality we know in life: the reality of God's love for us in Jesus Christ. Without the Spirit, this knowledge would be totally lost for us. The Spirit witnesses to us, pointing us toward our Lord and Savior, Jesus Christ. By the work of the Holy Spirit, the gospel message of Jesus Christ is applied to our lives, and we receive the gift of salvation.

The Spirit is at work in the world. The Holy Spirit brings life, the Spirit creates life and renews life. The Spirit's power is at work in the world, in every place, at every time. The Spirit gives power to the powerless; the Spirit enables works of justice and peace in the world. The Spirit fills the longings of the human heart. The Spirit is God with us, at work in ways we do not know, to carry out and fulfill God's ultimate plan and purposes for this world and for the whole cosmos.

The apostle Paul wrote, "If we live by the Spirit, let us also be guided by the Spirit" (Gal. 5:25). As Calvin put it, "If God's Spirit lives in us, let Him govern all our actions."[38] The Holy Spirit guides our lives. Our excitement in the Christian faith, and as Presbyterian Christians in the church, is seeing where and how God's Holy Spirit will lead and guide us—and seeing ways that the Holy Spirit is at work in this world!

Chapter 5

MINISTRY IN TODAY'S CULTURES

OUR MINISTRIES IN THE CHURCH OF JESUS CHRIST ARE marked by varying mixtures of joy and pain. Joys flood when events or programs succeed or when human problems are met and overcome. Pain proceeds from all those times when the waters are rough, the problems insurmountable, and the results unrecognizable. Then we may well wonder just what it really takes to be equipped for doing "the work of ministry" (Eph. 4:12).

A bit of reflection shows us that facile techniques can never ultimately see us through the ups and downs of ministry. Seminary educations for pastors do not provide all the answers. Denominational "program packets" don't last too long, and slick gimmicks give neither us nor our constituents all that is needed for ministry by the whole church to the whole world.

We all need to realize the theological foundations of ministry. We all need some approach, some grounding, some reflection that is sound and satisfying to help us understand and appropriate within ourselves what it means to do ministry and be the ministers of Jesus Christ we feel ourselves called to be. What is it that will help us keep on keeping on, when even our most "brilliant" or "innovative" programs fall flat on their faces in the local church? What is it that will keep us coming back again and again to the nursing home, the sick room, the funeral service month after month, year after year, throughout our ministries? What vision do we have of ministry to galvanize us to action in the midst of situations where the safest, most practical, and easiest course would simply be to stay still and keep quiet? The questions throng. Like it or not, they are persistent. The questions nag at us, tug at our elbows. These questions dog us even when we're dead tired. They won't be put to rest no matter how hard we try to shake them off.

So if we're at all sensitive, it behooves us to reflect on what we're up to in doing the work of ministry. We need a rationale—and not just our own rationale, something we convince ourselves of by ourselves and from ourselves—but something with depth and meaning. We need to know it is worth it and that what we're investing our lives in, the gospel ministry of Jesus Christ, does have in itself an ultimate significance. We need, in short, a theological foundation for our ministries. We need an understanding of who we are and what we do that is rooted in the rich soil of the gospel and is grounded in God. That alone can pull us through. That alone can help us stand and withstand our own changes in temperament and direction and even our changes in commitments to certain projects and goals through the years. We really do need to believe that the ministry of Jesus Christ is a basket strong enough to carry all our eggs!

There are a number of ways to establish the theological foundations for ministry. One can reflect biblically on the data found there. A study of church history would reveal differing patterns and understandings of ministry found at different times. Or theological thought can be given to what ministry means in the light of our understandings of God, humanity, Jesus Christ, the church, and so forth. Perhaps a combination of these approaches can serve to sketch the fundamentals of a theological foundation of ministry.

British New Testament scholar T. W. Manson provided a basic insight into ministry when he wrote,

> There is one "essential" ministry, the only ministry that is unchallengeably essential. That is the ministry which the Lord Jesus Christ opened in Galilee after John the Baptist had been put in prison, the ministry which He carried on in Galilee and Judaea, the ministry which He continues to this day in and through the Church, which is His body. . . . The Church is the Body of Christ; and the life of the Church is the continuation of the Messianic Ministry. It follows that the nature of the Church's task can be defined by reference to the records of the public career of Jesus, His teaching and His acts.[1]

From Manson's statements, three points emerge.

THE MINISTRY OF JESUS

When examining the foundations for our own ministries, we find first that all ministry derives from Jesus Christ. Jesus Christ is supremely the minister.

We may think this is rather obvious. Of course ministry comes from Christ. Who else would be the source of ministry? Who else could it be? We in the church are called "Christians." We bear the name "little Christs." It is around Jesus Christ that all worship revolves. So is it not obvious also that from him all ministry should originate?

While this may seem self-evident, it may also be obscured from our view for a couple of reasons. First, we may lose sight of Jesus as the source for ministry when we face the muddle of ministerial models before us.

Throughout the world, in its many cultures, we have thousands of local churches. As one observer put it about North America, in these churches, "Almost anything in the line of ministry can be found."[2] We see ministries to the very poor and to the very rich. We see street ministries, campus ministries, parish ministries, and a host of other specialized ministries. Even within these categories, ministry styles, agendas, and emphases vary widely. To whom can one go for guidelines and examples of what a minister "should be"? We are not long in the ministry before such things as "role models," "role expectations," and "role conflicts" begin to take on a significant place in our thoughts.

With such an amazing variety of ministerial options and roles open, we can feel the hassle of trying to find our place. As Richard Neuhaus described it,

> The minister is expected to be preacher, leader of worship, counselor, teacher, scholar, helper of the needy, social critic, administrator, revivalist, fund raiser, and a host of other sometimes impossible things. Pastors harassed by these conflicting expectations and claims upon time and ability are tempted to embark upon an open-ended game of trade-offs. Today I'll be a little of this and a little of that; tomorrow I'll be a little of the other thing and something else. For the conscientious who are determined to keep the game going, it is a certain formula for confusion and collapse.[3]

So we can be fragmented in our approach to ministry when the multiplicity of role models becomes muddled. We are left confused and bewildered.

A second reason we may lose sight of the fact that all ministry derives from Jesus Christ is that we tend to become obsessed with what we consider the various "inauthentic forms" of the church community that we serve.

Church is where it happens for us—if it happens at all. Yet we see much in the churches that is passed off as "Christian" when we have genuine doubts about the validity of that label. There are various mixtures of prejudice, racism, and sexism fused with the so-called old-time religion. We see loyalties to social position; wealth and privilege take over the place in people's lives where we think Jesus Christ should be. Can we bless these things? Can we baptize these forms of piety that churches and people wish to call authentic Christian faith? The temptation is always to go with the flow— to accommodate the message and to take our cue for ministry not primarily from our Lord but from our surroundings. Giving in to that urge is all too easy. We know, sadly enough, that all too often "whoever pays the preacher calls the sermon." Inauthentic forms of church community can cloud our vision of ministry as coming from Christ.

But Jesus is the true source of all ministry. Just as theologically we affirm that Jesus Christ is the head of the church, so also we need to keep before us the vision of Jesus as the source of all our efforts in ministry. To have a lesser view will ultimately leave us burned out and spiritually bankrupt.

The New Testament writings leave no doubt that the early church saw its ministry as growing and developing out of its commitment and obedience to Jesus Christ as its source, its head. Colossians 2:19 refers to "the head, *from whom* the whole body, nourished and held together by its ligaments and sinews, grows with a growth that is from God" (emphasis added). So also in Ephesians 4:15–16 we find, "But speaking the truth in love, we must grow up in every way into him who is the head, into Christ, *from whom* the whole body, joined and knit together by every ligament with which it is equipped, as each part is working properly, promotes the body's growth in building itself up in love" (emphasis added). The ministry of the church originates with Jesus Christ *from whom* all else flows. Early Christians saw ministry as rooted and grounded and issuing forth from the one who gives the church its own character: Jesus Christ himself.

All this, theologically, is connected with the varieties of New Testament images for the church. Paul Minear identified ninety-six such pictures in the New Testament.[4] But all of them assume that Christ is present and active in the church. Jesus Christ is present and active in the church as the Lord of the church.[5] So Jesus Christ is the source of power for our ministries. Ultimately our work and service in his name find their justification, their "success," their goal in him. For he is the one through whom the Holy Spirit calls us together as the people of God, the community of faith, the church of Jesus Christ. From Jesus Christ all ministry comes.

THE MINISTRY OF THE CHURCH

Second, our theological foundations for ministry rest partly on the belief that the ministry we carry on in the church is a continuation of the messianic ministry of Jesus.

When the post-resurrection church began at Pentecost, two factors were part of the Pentecost experience. The apostles were there representing the ministry of Christ. Their Master, who took the form of a servant and became obedient unto death, even the death of the cross, was now alive, having been raised by the power of God. The Holy Spirit was also present. The Spirit, promised by Jesus (John 14:26), was now given to the young church. This Spirit, who calls the church together (1 Cor. 12:3), is the one who brings believers even today into touch with the living Jesus Christ. So the ministry of the church and our own ministries within it are grounded in Jesus Christ as he is with his people through the Holy Spirit.

In a real sense, then, we can speak theologically, as Dietrich Bonhoeffer did, of "Christ existing as the

Church."[6] Bonhoeffer wrote, "The sole content of the church is in any case the revelation of God in Christ. He is present to the church in his Word, by which the community is constituted ever anew. The church is the presence of Christ, as Christ is the presence of God."[7] Christ is present to the church, with the church, and in the church. Through the church and its ministry, the messianic ministry begun by Jesus of Nazareth continues. This one essential ministry of Jesus Christ takes shape and historical form in this world through the ongoing work of those who believe in him. This concept led Karl Barth to call the church "the earthly-historical form of existence of Jesus Christ Himself." "Because He is," says Barth, "it is; it is because He is."[8] Or, as Robert S. Paul wrote, "It is my contention that the exercise of 'ministry' in word, deed, and presence is at the heart of all ecclesiology."[9]

In one sense, then, our own ministries are already defined for us. They are to move in the direction already set by the ministry of Jesus Christ. Christ is made known to men and women today through the ministry of the Christian church, its leadership and membership who re-present Christ to the world and set their agendas in light of Christ's agenda.

OUR OWN MINISTRIES

We come to the third insight of our original statement: All derivative ministries reflect the one essential ministry of Jesus Christ. Manson wrote, "It follows that the nature of the church's task can be defined by reference to the records of the public career of Jesus,

his teaching and his acts." In another work, Manson
said,

> All our ecclesiastical designs are to be tested against
> the master plan depicted in the gospel. All our
> endeavors are to be understood as ways in which the
> Risen Lord continues his work in the world. If we
> want to have right conceptions of the Church, what
> it is, and what it has to do here and now, there is one
> way and one way only by which we can get them,
> and that is by considering Jesus of Nazareth as he is
> portrayed for us in the gospels, what he is and what he
> does there and then.[10]

Thus, all our own derivative ministries must reflect the
original, essential ministry of Jesus. The character of
the church and the character of us who are the church's
ministers must be in harmony with and signposts of
the reign of God. The reign of God was the essential
proclamation and act of the God who lived among us
in Jesus Christ.[11]

Just as God reveals who God is by what God does,
so the church and we in our Christian ministries show
the world who we are by what we do. Our confessions
of faith must interpret our actions and our ministries;
our ministries must reflect our confessions of faith. In
the service for ordination of teaching and ruling elders
and deacons of the Presbyterian Church (U.S.A.), the
candidate is asked if he or she will "try to show the love
and justice of Jesus Christ." For ministers of Word and
Sacrament who are the church's teaching elders, this
question is posed in the same question that asks, "Will
you be a faithful teaching elder, proclaiming the good
news in Word and Sacrament, teaching faith and caring

for people?"[12] What one does in the world in showing "the love and justice of Jesus Christ" is inextricably joined to one's work in the ministry of proclamation, teaching faith, and caring for people. Word and deed interpret each other.

So our ministries, in all their many forms, are to reflect the life, ministry, and work of Jesus Christ as he is presented to us in Scripture. Yet what is being called for here is not simply an *imitatio Christi* (imitation of Christ). The spiritual classic by that name by Thomas á Kempis (*The Imitation of Christ*, c. 1418) has its rightful place. In the United States, some people think simplistically along the lines of Charles Sheldon's nineteenth-century classic novel, *In His Steps*. In the story, the guide for action for a whole town for a year was to be the question, "What would Jesus do" in this situation? The story tells the results of people asking that question. Yet actually this question is not enough for us. Today, in all our many cultures, we are separated by millennia, geography, and social location from the life lived by Jesus of Nazareth. To ask what Jesus would do today in cultures throughout the world would likely leave us baffled and perplexed. But what we need to capture to see our derivative ministries as reflecting the essential ministry of Jesus is the notion of *sequentia Christi*, that is, "the following of Christ." We today "come after" Christ. We are "followers" of Jesus. So the real question for us to ask in all our ministries is, "What would Jesus have me do in the situation at hand?" We are to follow in the directions Jesus points. Our ministries move toward the goals he established. They reflect his teachings and his acts in our own historical and cultural contexts.

ESSENTIAL CHARACTERISTICS OF THE MESSIANIC MINISTRY

What then are essential characteristics of the messianic ministry of Jesus Christ that our own life and work today reflect? It takes a lifetime of study and guidance by the Holy Spirit to know about Jesus Christ and even more to know what the will of God for us is where we are now in ministries that reflect Jesus Christ. But there are surely two characteristics or perspectives about the person and work of Jesus that stand out as crucial for our thoughts about the theological foundations of ministry.

Service. First, we reflect the messianic ministry of Jesus when we realize that Jesus Christ came among us primarily as a servant. The work he came to do was the work of service. As Mark 10:45 puts it, "For the Son of Man came not to be served but to serve, and to give his life a ransom for many." The King James Version renders it, "not to be ministered unto, but to minister." In the English language, the term "minister" is the word used to translate the Greek word *diakonos*, which means "servant," "helper," "deacon."[13]

This basic insight about Jesus Christ has set the tone for a number of writers on the church in recent times. What they have stressed is that the church's mission and ministry are to take on the character of its Lord. And Christ's ministry was one of *diakonia*—servant-hood. Writers as diverse as Karl Barth, J. C. Hoeken-dijk, and Robert S. Paul, as well as the Second Vatican Council, have made the point forcefully.[14] The concept of servanthood, which we translate as "ministry," is basic. As Hans Küng put it,

> It is not law or power, knowledge or dignity but service which is the basis of discipleship. The model for the disciples in their following of Christ is therefore not the secular ruler and not the learned scribe, nor even the priest who stands above his people (Jesus, remarkably enough, never once takes him as an example; cf. Hebrews); the only valid model is that of the [one] who serves at table: "But I am among you as one who serves (at table)" (Lk. 22:27).[15]

Thus, leadership or ministry in the reign of God is for those who are also willing to assume the servant posture. The willingness must be there to live without a home, wash another's feet, embrace the cross. Robert Paul has written that "there is no other pattern for the church. Insofar as it is not prepared to accept that pattern it is not the church of Jesus Christ; but insofar as it does, whatever its more formal theological shortcomings, it cannot be anything but the church of Jesus Christ."[16] So, theologically, our own ministries—whatever their specific shapes—reflect the one essential ministry of Jesus Christ, the one who came to serve and reconcile.

Reconciliation. Second, Jesus came to reconcile. Reconciliation is widely seen as a central motif of the gospel. In himself, Jesus Christ reconciles humanity to God and to one another. The Confession of 1967 of the Presbyterian Church (U.S.A.) states that "God's reconciling work in Jesus Christ and the mission of reconciliation to which he has called his church are the heart of

the gospel in any age."[17] This insight is based solidly on
the biblical witness of God's reconciling action in Jesus
Christ. John 3:16 speaks of God reconciling the world,
Matthew 5:24 of the reconciliation of peoples, 1 Corinthians 7:11 of husbands and wives, Ephesians 2:13–16
of nations and races, and Colossians 1:20 of the reconciliation of humanity and the whole cosmic order.

What does reconciliation mean? Richard Neuhaus
suggests that "reconciliation means transformation."
Further:

> Reconciliation is a dominant metaphor for ministry.
> Others expect us to be, and we likely expect ourselves
> to be, reconcilers. Unless our understanding of recon-
> ciliation flows from this biblical understanding of a
> life-transforming process, the idea of being a minister
> of reconciliation is, frankly, not very exciting. Without
> this theological vision that points us toward the com-
> ing Kingdom, reconciliation is little more than help-
> ing people to adjust. Ministers of reconciliation then
> become brokers of other people's problems, negoti-
> ating temporary settlements between sins in conflict.
> The danger is that reconciliation is perverted into
> conformation. "Do not be conformed to this world
> but be transformed by the renewal of your mind, that
> you may prove what is the will of God, what is good
> and acceptable and perfect" (Rom. 12). When we are
> helping people to cope by conforming rather than to
> change by transforming, when we make smooth the
> way of accommodation, when we relieve the tension
> between the actual and the real, then we have become
> reconcilers who have betrayed Christ's ministry of
> reconciliation.[18]

When we take our cue from Jesus we will seek the
transformation of relationships and structures in ways

that reflect the mind of Christ and that will have a lasting impact on groups and lives. Reconciliation reflects the person of Christ.

MINISTRY AND HOPE

Our ministries in the church of Jesus Christ and our personal ministries are nurtured by the theological foundations of ministry. We need these to keep us carrying out the ministerial tasks both corporately and personally. The ways our ministries are carried out will vary, of course, depending on our vocations, locations, and the contexts in which we minister. But we need these foundations to give us the grounding that enables us to keep on keeping on in ministry. When times are tough, we are sustained by the servant Jesus and the Christ who reconciles the world.

But one more element also pulls us ahead in our ministries. It is Christian hope. It is our hope in God through Jesus Christ by the power of the Holy Spirit. We need this hope to lift us above the setbacks and disappointments in ministry, corporately and personally, to fix our eyes on the end toward which we move— the ultimate establishment of the reign or kingdom of God. To this end, all our ministries are directed in the here and now, anticipating the kingdom that is to come.

John Calvin's words about hope can set us in the right direction. Calvin said that "hope is nothing else than the expectation of those things which faith has believed to have been truly promised by God. Thus, faith believes God to be true, hope awaits the time when his truth shall be manifested. . . . Faith is the foundation upon which hope rests, hope nourishes and sustains faith. . . . Hope refreshes faith, that it may not become weary. . . . Hope is nothing but the nourishment and strength of faith. . . . We look for the time when God will openly show that which is now hidden under hope."[19]

Our ministries are carried out by faith. Faith in Jesus Christ sends us into the world to minister in his name, in whatever cultures we find ourselves. Our faith is grounded in the triune God, the Creator God who guides us through providence in our lives. We minister in the name of Jesus Christ, by the power of the Holy Spirit. These are the theological realities to which Christian hope points. We do not have simple optimism or a feel-good feeling about our ministries. Our ministries are driven by faith that is nourished and sustained by hope. Karl Barth wrote, "As the Subject of the faith and love of the Christian, Jesus Christ is also the Subject of his hope."[20] Barth continued to say that "in hoping in Jesus Christ, the Christian hopes for the glory of God investing the whole creation of God of every time and place with unspotted and imperishable glory."[21]

To do ministry on behalf of Jesus Christ, nurtured by faith and grounded in hope, means that all our ministries will be carried out for the glory of God. This is what faith and hope point us toward: To do all things for the glory of God (1 Cor. 10:31). This is a Reformed impulse. This is a Christian impulse. Our lives are "hidden with Christ in God" (Col. 3:3) and we are to live—and to minister—to God's glory.

The fullness of God's glory will one day be revealed. "The earth will be filled with the knowledge of the glory of the LORD, as the waters cover the sea," promises the prophet Habbakuk (Hab. 2:14). In the book of Revelation, we are comforted by the sure promise that "the kingdom of the world has become the kingdom of our Lord and of his Messiah, and he will reign forever and ever" (Rev. 11:15). This is a destiny to dream about. This is a faith—and a hope—that can bring us through even our darkest hours. Our ministries are grounded in God's promise in Jesus Christ, the one who serves, the one who reconciles. We live into the hope of seeing that day when God is "all in all" (1 Cor. 15:28).

Glory be to the Father, and to the Son, and to the Holy Spirit. Amen.

Chapter 6

WHAT IT MEANS TO BE REFORMED

"What does it mean to be Reformed?" That question has many possible responses. The Reformed tradition has a long and rich history from early days in Europe, spreading to England and Scotland and then to America. This is to say nothing of the worldwide family of the Reformed, now found in all regions of the globe, in both the eastern and the western hemispheres. Our tradition is one that is "reformed and always being reformed"—in light of the Word of God. As God works among us and new insights emerge, our Reformed theology and Reformed faith are deepened and strengthened. So we are part of a vital, ongoing tradition that opens us to the work of God's Word and Spirit among us, in the world, in the church, and in our own lives. Our Reformed theological beliefs have implications for today's world. A Reformed faith that lives today is a perspective that is brought to bear on social, political, environmental, and religious issues. As Christians we are a minority people in the world. As Reformed Christians we are even more of a minority. But our theological traditions and our understandings of Scripture lead us to confess our Reformed faith and to confess it in the midst of today's world and all its problems.

Our Reformed tradition is a confessional tradition. As the followers of Zwingli and Calvin and Bullinger migrated throughout Europe and then beyond, they confessed their faith by writing confessions of faith. We have many examples and collections of the Christian faith confessed by the Reformed. These are local expressions of the Christian faith as those Reformed persons understood it. First, Reformed Christians identified themselves as members of the church catholic, the communion of saints spread throughout the world. Second, they saw themselves as members of distinctively Reformed bodies. They wanted to express what it meant to them to believe in God's truth and to say what the implications of that truth are for what they believed and how they lived. The earliest Christian confession was "Jesus Christ is Lord" (Phil. 2:11). All the derivative confessions down through history to the present day—and especially confessions of faith in the Reformed tradition—emerge from this confession as Reformed Christians seek to say and live what it means to be captive to the Lordship of Jesus Christ.

Reformed theology as it developed by theologians from the sixteenth century to today also seeks to express God's truth. Like confessions of faith themselves, Reformed theology has taken many forms. Yet, through all of the formulations of Reformed theology, the commitment is always present to expound the truth of God's Word and to understand the implications of that Word of God for the present world. Reformed theologians have seen this blending of theory and practice as inherent in the nature of theology itself. I did my doctoral dissertation on William Perkins (1558–1602), one of the leading English Puritan theologians during the sixteenth century. The Puritans as Reformed people sought to know not only what to believe but how to live as faithful Christians. William Perkins began one of his major works by defining theology as "the science of living blessedly for ever."[1] This phrase captures an essential impulse of the Reformed tradition. Theology is a practical science. What we believe affects our lives. How we live is guided by what we believe, so theology matters. Theology has an impact on human existence in terms of belief, but also in terms of action and the whole orientation of our lives. As John Calvin put it, "For the Word of God is not received by faith if it flits about in the top of the brain, but when it takes root in the depth of the heart."[2]

What follows is a look at one way of understanding what it means to be Reformed in light of the faith of the holy catholic church and of the Christian doctrines that churches have confessed through the centuries. In light of the nature of our Reformed confessions and Reformed theology, we can also explore some of the implications for our Reformed faith for today's world.

GOD'S REVELATION IN SCRIPTURE

Reformed confessions from the sixteenth century very often began with an article on Holy Scripture. These articles indicated the nature of Scripture and established it as the foundation for the theological understandings that followed. This approach was in contrast to Lutheran confessions, which more often assumed the authority of Scripture without devoting a separate article to it.

Characteristic of the Reformed approach is the Second Helvetic Confession (1566), written by Heinrich Bullinger (1504–1575). Chapter 1 is titled "Of the Holy Scripture Being the True Word of God." Much is packed into the two opening paragraphs, and they bear hearing in themselves:

> We believe and confess the canonical Scriptures of the holy prophets and apostles of both Testaments to be the true Word of God, and to have sufficient authority of themselves, not of men. For God himself spoke to the fathers, prophets, apostles, and still speaks to us through the Holy Scriptures.
>
> And in this Holy Scripture, the universal Church of Christ has the most complete exposition of all that pertains to a saving faith, and also to the framing of a life acceptable to God; and in this respect it is expressly commanded by God that nothing be either added to or taken from the same.[3]

The Bible is God's revelation of who God is and what God has done.

Word of God. Notice the important elements in this Reformed confession on the nature of Holy Scripture. First, the Scriptures of both the Old and the New

Testament are "the true Word of God." In harmony with the early church, the Reformed have always recognized that our faith turns to both the Old Testament and the New Testament as the "true Word of God."

Scripture here is identified as the "Word of God." It is the expression of the triune God—Father, Son, and Holy Spirit. Scripture is the Word of God because it is God's revelation, God's self-communication. As a document of the Presbyterian Church (U.S.A.) put it, "It is a central feature of the church's experience of revelation that we hear the voice of the living God speaking to us in the canonical books of Scripture."[4] As Karl Barth put it, "The divine Word is the divine speaking."[5] God revealed who God is to the people of Israel in the Old Testament and to the people of the church in the New Testament—where God is revealed definitively in the person of Jesus Christ. We call the Bible God's "special revelation" because it conveys a knowledge of God that we could not gain elsewhere— nowhere else.

Authority of Scripture. The Second Helvetic Confession goes on to say that the Scriptures have "sufficient authority of themselves and not of men." We hear in the background here the debate with Roman Catholicism about the relation of Scripture to the church and to church tradition. Against the Roman view of the dual authority of church and tradition, the Protestant Reformers asserted the sole authority of Scripture (Lat. *sola scriptura*) in that the Scriptures alone are the locus of authority for Christian churches. So Bullinger here asserts the singular authority of Scripture over all other "authorities," meaning that the Bible possesses a unique authority for the church's life and the life of the Christian. As the Presbyterian Church (U.S.A.) document states, "It is a central teaching of the Reformed tradition that the Bible is uniquely authoritative as a medium of revelation—and particularly that more recent expressions of a tradition of the church cannot have a similar status."[6]

Inspiration of Scripture. Scripture is authoritative for the church because, as Bullinger then says, "For God himself spoke to the fathers, prophets, apostles, and still speaks to us through the Holy Scriptures." Scripture is authoritative because it comes from God. Basic to this understanding is that Scripture is inspired by God (2 Tim. 3:16; 2 Pet. 1:21). The "inspiration of Scripture" means that God used human beings to communicate the divine message to be told to the world. The Holy Spirit enabled human words to become the "Word of God." How this has happened is a mystery. Reformed theology has affirmed both God's initiation of the process of inspiration through the Holy Spirit as well as the full freedom of those who wrote Scripture to write as the human persons they were, consistent with their historical contexts and fully as persons who lived in specific times and places. Scripture is inspired by God.

Faith and Life. Finally, as the Second Helvetic Confession says, "In this Holy Scripture, the universal Church of Christ has the most complete exposition of all that pertains to a saving faith, and also to the framing of a life acceptable to God." Notice here the confession of the Bible as providing the means of coming to "saving faith" and its authority to show us how to live a "life acceptable to God." Theology, again, is a practical science—the blending of faith and action, theology and ethics. This emphasis is picked up about a century later in the seventeenth-century Westminster Confession, which lists the books of Scripture and then says, "All which are given by inspiration of God, to be the rule of faith and life."[7]

So the Reformed affirm the Scriptures of the Old and New Testaments as the true Word of God, as authoritative, inspired, and our source for coming to saving faith in Jesus Christ and for living a life of faith unto God.

Scripture Today. In today's pluralistic world, these Reformed basics can still be held as crucial. In the midst of many sources of authority that cry out for attention all around us—political authorities, social authorities, the authority of certain celebrities or famous people—Reformed Christians focus on the authority of the Bible. Through the Scriptures we come to know God and God's Son, Jesus Christ, who is Lord of all. No other person or place provides this knowledge of God. The message of Reformed faith is that there is a sure and reliable source for our knowledge of God: the Scriptures of the Old and New Testaments. We may dialogue with and listen and learn from the insights of other religious faiths or viewpoints. But all they have to say ultimately needs to be understood in light of the church's Scriptures as the means through which God is revealed, as in no other way or place. The Bible is central for Reformed faith today. The Bible is the source of it all. The Bible tells us who God is, what God has done, and how God wants us to live. It is our source for theology and ethics, our source for salvation and the life of faith.

THE GOOD CREATOR

The God who is revealed in Scripture is the great God, the creator of the whole of reality. God is, as the ancient Nicene Creed puts it, "the Father Almighty, Maker of heaven and earth, and of all things visible and invisible."[8] This confession reflects the first words of Genesis: "In the beginning God created the heavens and the earth" (Gen. 1:1 RSV).

God is the creator, and the world is created. What does knowing this convey about what we know about God, our knowledge of God? Dutch theologian Hendrikus Berkhof, in the last century, answered the question this way: "The answer must be that in holy love God has decided to live with a reality outside God's self, a reality that as created is of a totally different order. It has pleased God to make this reality share in the glory and love of God's own being."[9]

When we look around us at the created reality, we may be filled with wonder and awe—when we see the beauty and grandeur of nature. But we may also be greatly afraid—when we see earthquakes, typhoons, and tsunamis. Yet the Scriptures proclaim and Reformed Christians affirm the account in Genesis: "God saw everything that he had made, and indeed, it was very good" (Gen. 1:31). As Berkhof puts it, "If created reality, which can enrapture but also frighten us, has its sole source of being in the initiative of the Father of Jesus Christ, then, in spite of everything, it must be a good thing. Creation is good because the Creator is good."[10] John Calvin called God "the fountain of every good."[11]

The Ecological Crisis. This view of God and the creation has a number of important implications, especially in light of the ecological crisis that our world faces today as one of its most crucial problems. There are many roots to this crisis. One theologian has summarized them as follows:

- *Anthropocentrism*—The view of the world that sees everything as existing primarily to serve humankind.
- *Power as domination*—The misuse of power in science and technology so that the desire to subject nature to human will becomes primary.
- *Denial of interconnectedness*—Respect for non-human forms of life and an individualism that does not care for the ecological balances of nature, feeding anthropocentrism and power as domination.
- *Assumption of limitless resources*—The view that clean air, pure water, and fertile fields are unlimited or always renewable, underlying the exploitation of the earth for human purposes.
- *Unchecked consumerism*—Recklessly consuming as much of the earth's resources as possible while millions of others lack even the basic necessities of life.[12]

Good Creator and Good Creation. In the face of all these attitudes and actions, Reformed faith asserts the good creator and the good creation. Seeing the relationship between creator and creation as well as creator and creature orients us toward ways of honoring and preserving the earth, toward seeing humans as God's servants and not as the ultimate, dominant source of power. To seek to bring all things under God's will and not under human will counters the power of domination that is rampant around us. To respect and nurture the web of life, seeing that all things are created good by the good God, removes us from a radical individualism toward a desire for an ecological unity in which the human family is seen as inhabiting the whole *oikoumenē* or "household" of creation and in which we seek to live with each other as responsible members of the family of God. Being good stewards of the good creation and recognizing the goodness of the Lord of creation will also lead us to seek renewable resources for all the earth's people and to provide them with the basic necessities of life.

The good creator has created a good creation. All within creation is "structurally good and important," as Berkhof puts it. He expands on this and also goes on to say that "createdness not only means that everything is good but also and for that reason that nothing is absolute. Nothing is less than a creature of God, but nothing is more than a creature of God either." There is an implied "fundamental unity of the world. More basic than the diversity of nations, races, and cultures is their unity. And more basic than the difference in matter and spirit, body and soul, nature and existence is their oneness."[13] A Reformed faith that is vital for today will recapture these emphases on the good creator and the good creation, in the face of our ecological crisis and also in the face of our nationalisms and desire for enemies, which tear at the fabric of the human family and the creatures created by the good God.

THE SAVIOR WHO REDEEMS

Seriousness of Sin. The good Creator created a good creation, but humans are fallen creatures. The Bible as well as Reformed Christianity have seen the utter seriousness of sin, which is our transgression, our alienation, our turning away from our good creator to the wants and desires of our own human hearts without regard to the will and purposes of our Creator God. The attitudes mentioned as contributing to our planet's ecological crisis are attitudes rooted in the human heart.

The anthropocentrism that sees all things as existing to serve humankind can be personalized as the story of each human creature. We live according to our own wills and desires, not God's. This the Bible calls sin.

The power of domination that subjects all things to the human will is also our personal desire for power in every arena of our existence.

Our denial of interconnectedness is our selfish individualism in which we seek only our own good and not the good of others.

All these and more can be biblical and theological images of sin.

The Reformed take sin and its power seriously. The Christian doctrine of original sin, which indicates that humans are sinful in their origins and their beginnings, has been seen by Reformed Christians as having a pervasive power through all areas of human life. Humans are sinners by nature. As Calvin said, "All parts of the soul were possessed by sin after Adam deserted the fountain of righteousness." Humans possess a corrupt nature, so that "the mind is given over to blindness and the heart to depravity."[14]

This situation is serious. Calvin continued by saying that the whole person is "overwhelmed—as by a deluge—from head to foot, so that no part is immune from sin and all that proceeds from [the person] is to be imputed to sin."[15] Calvin agreed with Luther, who, in his controversy with Erasmus over "free will," argued that the human will is bound in captivity to sin and is unable in itself to will to choose the good—that is, to choose to accept the gospel of Jesus Christ. So our wills are in "bondage" to the power of sin. We cannot, by ourselves, either "initiate" the way to salvation or "cooperate" with grace along the way to bring us to faith and ultimately to salvation in Jesus Christ. The theological "misery" that sin has caused is so total, so drastic, and so terrible that it leads to death, as Paul wrote to the Romans: "The wages of sin is death" (Rom. 6:23).

Person and Work of Christ. But there is more to Paul's verse. Paul's complete statement is, "The wages of sin is death, but the free gift of God is eternal life in Christ Jesus our Lord" (Rom. 6:23). This is the good news, the gospel of our Lord Jesus Christ.

Reformed Christians, along with all orthodox Christians, have seen Jesus Christ as God incarnate. The incarnation means, "The Word became flesh" (John 1:14), which Karl Barth called "the central New Testament statement."[16] As Calvin said, "God is comprehended in Christ alone."[17] God has sent Jesus Christ, the eternal Son of God, into the world to provide redemption and salvation—to create a new humanity out of fallen, sinful creatures. As Paul put it, "God proves his love for us in that while we still were sinners Christ died for us" (Rom. 5:8) and then, again, "In Christ God was reconciling the world to himself" (2 Cor. 5:19).

Classically, the Reformed have affirmed with the Christian church that "fully human, fully God,"[18] Jesus Christ is the second person of the Trinity: "fully God," but he is also a human, just like us in all ways—except for sin. The First Helvetic Confession (1536) says that Jesus Christ has "two distinct, unmixed natures in one single, indissoluble Person."[19] Theologians speak of a "hypostatic union," or a union of the two natures in the one person of Jesus Christ. What this means is, as Daniel Migliore has put it, "God acts, suffers, and triumphs in and through Jesus. In Jesus Christ we do not have less than God's very own presence in our humanity. In this person the eternal God suffers and acts for our salvation."[20]

The person of Christ is essential for the work of Christ. If Jesus Christ were not "fully human," he could not completely take on our needs as human beings. If Jesus Christ were not "fully God," his death would not have the power to save us. The church's concern for affirming the person of Jesus Christ as "fully God and fully human" is a concern for our salvation. If Jesus Christ were less than who the church proclaims, he could not redeem us from the power of sin and bring God's new humanity into existence. Put another way, as Migliore says, "No human being alone can save us. If Jesus Christ is not God with us, if the life and forgiveness that he offers are not God's own life and forgiveness, if his self-giving, sacrificial love poured out for our sake is not God's own love, then he cannot be Savior and Lord. Christian faith cannot compromise either on the full humanity or on the full deity of Jesus Christ."[21]

The person of Christ points us to the work of Christ, particularly the work of salvation. The Reformed, classically, have seen the work of Christ as an expression of his threefold office of prophet, priest, and king.[22] Christ as "prophet" teaches "perfect doctrine," conveys "perfect wisdom" to us.[23] Christ the "king" reigns over us—in the church and in the world—so that we are never left "destitute," since Christ the King will "provide for our needs until, our warfare ended, we are called to triumph."[24] Christ as "priest" is our "everlasting intercessor" who by "the sacrifice of his death" has "blotted out our own guilt and made satisfaction for our sins [Heb. 9:22]." Christ was both "priest and sacrifice."[25] In Christ's death, said Calvin, God "loved us even when we practiced enmity toward him and committed wickedness."[26] God has acted "to take away all cause for enmity and to reconcile us utterly to himself"; God wipes out "all evil in us by the expiation set forth in the death of Christ; that we, who were previously unclean and impure, may show ourselves righteous and holy in his sight."[27] This is salvation. This is the work of the Savior who redeems us. Our sin is forgiven, and sinners have a new standing in the sight of God, through the work of Jesus Christ.

Reformed theology has never adopted only one way of understanding the atonement—the death of Jesus Christ on the cross and how the death of Christ can save us, forgive our sin, and reconcile us to God. Many biblical images are used to describe the experience of "salvation." Like the Christian church as a whole, the Reformed have honored the wide variety of biblical descriptions of the work of Christ in his death on the cross and the forgiveness and redemption it brings. The work of Jesus Christ in salvation is made possible because of the person of Christ, who he is: truly human, truly divine.

The power of God, at work in Jesus Christ as prophet, priest, and king, is capsulized and focused in the resurrection of Jesus Christ. Paul said in Romans 1:4 that Jesus Christ "was declared to be Son of God with power according to the spirit of holiness by resurrection from the dead." Barth said that "the resurrection of Jesus Christ is the great verdict of God, the fulfillment and proclamation of God's decision concerning the event of the cross."[28] Christ's death and resurrection go together. Calvin distinguished them this way: "Through his death, sin was wiped out and death extinguished; through his resurrection, righteousness was restored and life raised up, so that—thanks to his resurrection—his death manifested its power and efficacy in us."[29] The innocent victim, Jesus Christ—who was put to death as the expression of the worst evil that could be carried out—became the victor when God raised him from the dead. The Brief Statement of Faith of the Presbyterian Church (U.S.A.) puts it this way:

Jesus was crucified,
   suffering the depths of human pain
   and giving his life for the sins of the world.
God raised this Jesus from the dead,
   vindicating his sinless life,
   breaking the power of sin and evil,
   delivering us from death to life eternal.[30]

Jesus Christ is the Savior who redeems us by his death and resurrection.

Jesus Christ Today. We live in a religiously pluralistic world. The great world religions may acknowledge Jesus Christ as a great man, a wise teacher, or an important prophet. But Reformed Christians proclaim that Jesus Christ is more than these things. We proclaim him as the eternal Son of God who lived and died and was raised again by the power of God to bring salvation to us and to the world. This is the message of the Christian gospel, a message that takes its place among the messages of all other world religions. Jesus is unique, we confess. He is a human person but also "more than a person." He is the second member of the Trinity, the eternal Word of God who was in the beginning "with God" (John 1:1). Even more, this Word "became flesh and lived among us" (John 1:14). He has come into this world to bring us salvation—forgiveness of sin and reconciliation with God. Jesus Christ is Christianity's unique center. As Barth said, "The history of salvation is first and last, at its center and in its origin, the history of Jesus Christ."[31] We respect, listen to, and learn from other religious faiths today. But we also confess, witness, and proclaim the gospel of the Christian faith: Jesus Christ is Lord and Savior.

THE SPIRIT OF LIFE

All this is known to us by the work of the Holy Spirit. One dimension of what it means to be Reformed is to have a robust view of the Holy Spirit. The Holy Spirit is active in both the church and the world. The Holy Spirit as "the power at work within us is able to accomplish abundantly far more than all we can ask or imagine" (Eph. 3:20).

The Spirit in the Church. Reformed theology emphasizes that we are given the gift of salvation by faith. It is the Holy Spirit who gives us faith. Calvin said, "Faith is the principal work of the Holy Spirit."[32] Since salvation is a gift of God's grace, the Reformed have emphasized God's election or predestination as the source of our salvation. God has chosen us and given us the gift of faith. God has chosen us in Christ, as Paul said, "before the foundation of the world" (Eph. 1:4). Calvin believed that in election God wants us to "contemplate nothing but his mere goodness."[33] For election is "the mother of faith"[34] in which "mercy alone appears on every side."[35] Where does salvation come from, asked Calvin, "but from God's election"?[36] Election brings an "inestimable fruit of comfort"[37] since Jesus Christ is the "mirror" of our election[38] and through the gift of faith by the Holy Spirit we may "embrace Christ, who is graciously offered to us and comes to meet us. He will reckon us in his flock and enclose us within his fold."[39]

Our election is expressed in our salvation or our justification. Those who are called by God or are the "elect of God" constitute the church of God. The Reformed, going back to Calvin, have always had a comprehensive view of the church. Calvin defined the church as including "not only the saints presently living on earth, but all the elect from the beginning of the world."[40] This is the all-inclusive "communion of saints." The visible church as we know it today is the body of those who are reconciled to God in Jesus Christ and who are, as the Confession of 1967 puts it, "sent into the world as [God's] reconciling community. This community, the church universal is entrusted with God's message of reconciliation and shares [God's] labor of healing the enmities which separate [people] from God and from each other. Christ has called the church to this mission and given it the gift of the Holy Spirit."[41] As *The Book of Order* of the Presbyterian Church (U.S.A.) puts it,

> The mission of God in Christ gives shape and substance to the life and work of the Church. In Christ, the Church participates in God's mission for the transformation of creation and humanity by proclaiming to all people the good news of God's love, offering to all people the grace of God at font and table, and calling all people to discipleship in Christ. Human beings have no higher goal in life than to glorify and enjoy God now and forever, living in covenant fellowship with God and participating in God's mission.[42]

The Holy Spirit goes on, as the Confession of 1967 states, to give gifts to the church to enable it to fulfill its service to God in the world. These gifts are preaching and teaching, praise and prayer, baptism and the Lord's Supper. While these gifts remain, says the Confession, "The church is obliged to change the forms of its service in ways appropriate to different generations and cultures."[43] Reformed theology has explored all these gifts of the Spirit given to the church.

On the personal level, the Holy Spirit gives gifts appropriate to our sanctification, our growth in faith as the outworking of our justification. Corporately, in the church, the Holy Spirit is God present with the church, enabling it to carry out mission and ministry according to God's will. Churches exist in diverse forms, but the Holy Spirit is the Spirit of unity who binds all the churches together. As Calvin put it, "The church universal is a multitude gathered from all nations; it is divided and dispersed in separate places, but agrees on the one truth of divine doctrine, and is bound by the bond of the same religion."[44]

The Spirit in the World. Reformed Christians today recognize the work of the Holy Spirit in the church. Do we also recognize the work of the Spirit in the world? From the beginning, the Spirit is the "spirit of life." God breathed into the nostrils of the first human "the breath of life; and the man became a living being" (Gen. 2:7). This spirit of life, the Spirit of God, is at work in the world. As Migliore writes,

> A Christian theology of the work of the Holy Spirit must not be confined to the life and witness of the church. There is a cosmic dimension of the work of the Spirit. If the Spirit is like the wind that "blows where it wills" (John 3:8), we must expect and be open to the working of the Spirit beyond the walls of the church. The Spirit of God is present and at work in the world of nature, in the restlessness of the human heart, in the work for justice and harmony in human relations, in the search for truth in the sciences, in the

skills of creative artists, and in the histories of the world religions.[45]

The Spirit Today. This is a challenge for a Reformed faith that lives today: How and where do we see the Holy Spirit of God at work to bring life, peace, hope, joy, and salvation? The church carries out mission and ministry. As Christians we each have our vocation or calling to live as faithful disciples of Jesus Christ.[46] The Holy Spirit supports and nurtures and brings new life to us all. One of our challenges as Reformed Christians is to "listen to what the Spirit is saying to the churches" (Rev. 2:7). Where do we find the Holy Spirit at work? How do we follow the leading of the Spirit, in the church and in our own lives? In what ways will we cooperate with the Holy Spirit of God as the Spirit is at work beyond the church, in the world? Reformed Christians and Reformed churches must respond to the work of the Holy Spirit who brings life!

REFORMED FAITH TODAY

We have seen some of what it means to be Reformed today. We have seen that Reformed Christians confess our faith. We look to the Bible as the authority for our Reformed faith. Our faith proclaims a good creator, a savior who redeems, and the Spirit of life who is at work in the church and the world.

We seek to live faithfully as Reformed Christians and people of the church. We will fail along our ways. We will need forgiveness. We will need God's power, help, and love. But through it all, Reformed Christians are people of hope. We live out our faith in the church. The church carries out its mission and ministry, trusting in the good Creator, the Savior who redeems, and the Spirit of life. Our vision is captured in the Confession of 1967:

> With an urgency born of this hope, the church applies itself to present tasks and strives for a better world. It does not identify limited progress with the kingdom of God on earth, nor does it despair in the face of disappointment and defeat. In steadfast hope, the church looks beyond all partial achievement to the final triumph of God.[47]

Amen!

NOTES

Chapter 1: The Bible

1. See Donald K. McKim, *The Bible in Theology and Preaching*, rpt. (Eugene, OR: Wipf & Stock Publishers, 1999), for a discussion of major views about the nature of the Bible.

2. The Presbyterian Church (U.S.A.), *Book of Confessions: Study Edition* (Louisville, KY: Geneva Press, 1999), 5.001.

3. Heinrich Bullinger, *Summa Christenlicher Religion* (Zurich: Christoffel Froschouwer, 1576), cited in Edward A. Dowey Jr., *A Commentary on the Confession of 1967 and Introduction to the Book of Confessions* (Philadelphia: Westminster Press, 1966), 204–5.

4. On this topic, see Presbyterian Church (U.S.A.), "The Nature of Revelation in the Christian Tradition from a Reformed Perspective," in *Major Themes in the Reformed Tradition*, ed. Donald K. McKim, rpt. (Eugene, OR: Wipf & Stock Publishers, 1998), 35–50.

5. See Martin Luther, *Prefaces to the Old Testament* in *Luther's Works*, ed. E. Theodore Bachman, trans. Helmut T. Lehmann (Philadelphia: Fortress Press, 1960), 35:235; and his *A Brief Instruction on What to Look for and Expect in the Gospels*, 35:121.

6. See Jack B. Rogers and Donald K. McKim, *The Authority and Interpretation of the Bible: An Historical Approach*, rpt. (Eugene, OR: Wipf & Stock Publishers, 1999). The Task Force on Biblical Authority and Interpretation report can be found at http://cayugasyracuse.org/files/2913/2805/0667/Presbyterian_Use__Understanding_of_Holy_Scripture.pdf.

7. John Calvin, *Institutes of the Christian Religion* 1.7.4; ed. John T. McNeill, trans. Ford Lewis Battles, LCC (Philadelphia: Westminster Press, 1960), 79.

Chapter 2: The God Who Creates and Provides

1. The Presbyterian Church (U.S.A.), *Book of Confessions: Study Edition* (Louisville, KY: Geneva Press, 1999), 5.032, citing Ps. 33:6.

2. See, for example, my telling of it in Donald K. McKim, *Theological Turning Points: Major Issues in Christian Thought* (Atlanta: John Knox Press, 1988), ch. 1.

3. "The Tetrapolitan Confession of 1530," in *Reformed Confessions of the 16th Century*, ed. Arthur C. Cochrane with a new Introduction by Jack Rogers (Louisville, KY: Westminster John Knox Press, 2003), 56.

4. "The First Helvetic Confession of Faith of 1536," in ibid., 101.

5. *Book of Confessions* 10.1.

6. Ibid., 7.117.

7. Ibid., 4.026. A contemporary translation of the answer is:

> That the eternal Father of our Lord Jesus Christ,
> who out of nothing created heaven and earth
> and everything in them,[1]
> who still upholds and rules them
> by his eternal counsel and providence,[2]
> is my God and Father
> because of Christ the Son.[3]

I trust God so much that I do not doubt
he will provide
whatever I need
for body and soul,[4]
and will turn to my good
whatever adversity he sends upon me
in this sad world.[5]
God is able to do this because he is almighty God[6]
and desires to do this because he is a faithful Father.[7]

[1] Gen. 1; Ps. 33:6
[2] Ps. 104; 115:3; Matt. 10:29; Heb. 1:3
[3] John 1:12; Rom. 8:15; Gal. 4:5–7; Eph. 1:5
[4] Ps. 55:22; Matt. 6:25–26; Luke 12:22
[5] Rom. 8:28
[6] Rom. 10:12
[7] Matt. 6:32; 7:9

This translation is found at http://www.pcusa.org/media/uploads/oga/pdf/amendments_220_part1.pdf.

8. *Calvin's New Testament Commentaries*, 12 vols., ed. David W. Torrance and Thomas F. Torrance, trans. T. H. L. Parker, rpt. (Grand Rapids: Eerdmans, 1979), *Commentary 1 John 4:9* (CNTC 5:290).

9. *Calvin's New Testament Commentaries*, 12 vols., ed. David W. Torrance and Thomas F. Torrance, trans. William B. Johnston (Grand Rapids: Eerdmans, 1963), *Commentary on Hebrews 1:2* (CNTC 12:6–7).

10. Jürgen Moltmann, *God in Creation: A New Theology of Creation and the Spirit of God*, trans. Margaret Kohl (San Francisco: Harper & Row, 1985), 97–98.

11. Ibid., 229.

12. Calvin, *Institutes* 1.16.4.

13. Ibid.

14. See Benjamin Wirt Farley, "The Providence of God in Reformed Perspective," in *Major Themes in the Reformed Tradition*, ed. Donald K. McKim, rpt. (Eugene, OR: Wipf & Stock Publishers, 1998), 87–93.

15. Henry Hallam Tweedy, "Eternal God, Whose Power Upholds," *The Presbyterian Hymnal*, ed. LindaJo H. McKim (Louisville, KY: Westminster/John Knox Press, 1990), #412.

16. William Cowper, "O God, in a Mysterious Way," in ibid., #270.

17. Calvin, *Institutes* 1.17.2.

18. Ibid., 17.7.

19. Ibid., 1.17.11.

20. Ibid.

Chapter 3: Confessing Jesus Christ Today

1. *Book of Confessions: Study Edition* (Louisville, KY: Geneva Press, 1999), 3.06; cf. 5.066; 5.078.

2. Ibid., 5.077.

3. Ibid., 4.029; 4.030.

4. Jan Rohls, *Reformed Confessions: Theology from Zurich to Barmen*, trans. John Hoffmeyer, Columbia Series in Reformed Theology (Louisville, KY: Westminster John Knox Press, 1997), 102.

5. See my discussion in Donald K. McKim, *Theological Turning Points: Major Issues in Christian Thought* (Atlanta: John Knox Press, 1988), 74–85.

6. For a thorough survey of views about the theology of the atonement, see H. D. McDonald, *The Atonement of the Death of Christ: In Faith, Revelation, and History* (Grand Rapids: Baker Book House, 1985). McDonald's discussion of theologians in the Reformed tradition is excerpted in "Models of the Atonement in Reformed Theology," in *Major Themes in the Reformed Tradition*, ed. Donald K. McKim, rpt. (Eugene, OR: Wipf & Stock Publishers, 1998), 117–31.

7. *Book of Confessions* 8.11.

8. Ibid., 9.08.

9. Ibid., 10.2.

10. Ibid., 9.09.

11. Dutch Reformed theologian Herman Bavinck (1854–1921) made this point well: "Scripture alone is trustworthy in and of itself ([Gr.] *autopistos*), unconditionally binding us to faith and obedience, unchanging; a confession, on the other hand, always remains examinable and revisable by the standard of Scripture." See Herman Bavinck, *Reformed Dogmatics:*

Abridged in One Volume, ed. John Bolt (Grand Rapids: Baker Academic, 2011), 634.

12. See Presbyterian Church (U.S.A.), "The Confessional Nature of the Church" (1986), in *Major Themes in the Reformed Tradition*, ed. Donald K. McKim, rpt. (Eugene, OR: Wipf & Stock, 1998), 19–27; and Edward A. Dowey Jr., "Confessional Documents as Reformed Hermeneutic," 28–34.

13. I have developed these ideas more fully in "Reformed Convictions and Religious Pluralism," in *Many Voices, One God: Being Faithful in a Pluralistic World*, ed. Walter Brueggemann and George W. Stroup (Louisville, KY: Westminster John Knox Press, 1998), 78–92.

14. *Book of Confessions* 5.007.

15. Karl Barth, *Church Dogmatics*, II/2, ed. G. W. Bromiley and T. F. Torrance, trans. G. W. Bromiley et al. (Edinburgh: T. & T. Clark, 1957), 417.

16. Donald G. Bloesch, *Jesus Is Victor! Karl Barth's Doctrine of Salvation* (Nashville: Abingdon, 1976), 62.

17. Frederick William Faber, "There's a Wideness in God's Mercy," *The Presbyterian Hymnal*, ed. LindaJo H. McKim (Louisville, KY: Westminster/John Knox Press, 1990), #298. Faber was born to Calvinist parents, was ordained in the Church of England, and became a Roman Catholic priest. He was a priest when he wrote the text of this hymn. The first stanza is, "There's a wideness in God's mercy, like the wideness of the sea; there's a kindness in God's justice, which is more than liberty. There is no place where earth's sorrows are more felt than up in heaven; there is no place where earth's failings have such kindly judgment given."

18. *Book of Confessions* 4.001.

19. Ibid., 5.077.

Chapter 4: The Holy Spirit in Church and World

1. Frederick Dale Bruner and William Hordern, *The Holy Spirit: Shy Member of the Trinity* (Minneapolis: Augsburg Publishing House, 1984).

2. The most thorough treatment of the Holy Spirit is Anthony C. Thiselton, *The Holy Spirit—In Biblical Teaching, through the Centuries, and Today* (Grand Rapids: Eerdmans, 2013).

3. See The Presbyterian Church (U.S.A.), *Book of Confessions: Study Edition* (Louisville, KY: Geneva Press, 1999), 1.1–3. The Western church included the phrase "and the Son" (Lat. *filioque*) to the creed to express its theological understanding that the Spirit "proceeds" from both God the Father and God the Son. Eastern theologians disagreed. The issue became one of the reasons for the split between the Western and Eastern churches in 1054.

4. John Calvin, *Institutes of the Christian Religion* 3.2.33, ed. John T. McNeill, trans. Ford Lewis Battles, LCC (Philadelphia: Westminster Press, 1960), 580.

5. Ibid., 1.7.4.

6. Ibid.

7. Ibid.

8. Ibid., 1.7.5.

9. Ibid., 3.1.1.

10. Ibid., 3.2.34.

11. Ibid., 3.1.2.

12. Ibid., 3.1.4. The quotes in this paragraph are from *Institutes* 3.1.4.

13. William C. Placher, *The Triune God: An Essay in Postliberal Theology* (Louisville, KY: Westminster John Knox Press, 2007), 83.

14. Karl Barth, *Church Dogmatics,* IV/2, trans. G. W. Bromiley (Edinburgh: T. & T. Clark, 1958), 654. (Hereafter cited as *CD.*)

15. Karl Barth, *Church Dogmatics*, I/1, trans. G.W. Bromiley, rpt. (Edinburgh: T.&T. Clark, 1980), 474.

16. This has historically been true of Pentecostal traditions. See Thiselton, *Holy Spirit*, 57–62.

17. Calvin, *Institutes* 3.2.35.

18. This point is developed by the Roman Catholic theologian Hans Küng in *The Church*, trans. Ray and Rosaleen Ockenden (New York: Sheed and Ward, 1967), 150–203.

19. Ibid., 175, 176.

20. As the Ephesians passage makes clear, we are elect "in Christ." That is, God "chose us in Christ" (Eph. 1:4) and it is the gift of faith in Christ, given by the Holy Spirit, that is the expression and sign of our election or salvation. The elect are the people of God or the church. As Bavinck said, "To be elect 'in Christ' is to be organically united to his body, the church" (Herman Bavinck, *Reformed Dogmatics: Abridged in One Volume*, ed. John Bolt [Grand Rapids: Baker Academic, 2011], 262). Cf. Lewis B. Smedes, "Being in Christ," in *Major Themes in the Reformed Tradition*, ed. Donald K. McKim, rpt. (Eugene, OR: Wipf & Stock Publishers, 1998), 150–52.

21. Calvin, *Institutes* 3.24.4.

22. Ibid.

23. Ibid., 3.3.21.

24. Ibid., 3.3.6. A distinctive emphasis in Reformed theology is that regeneration is prior to faith. God calls us (elects us), makes us a new creation, and gives us the gift of faith by the work of the Holy Spirit. As Bavinck put it, "The Reformed insisted on regeneration as prior, acknowledging the Holy Spirit as the agent moving the human will before any act of its own" (*Reformed Dogmatics*, 498–99). "The purpose of regeneration," he continued, "is to make us spiritual people, those who live and walk by the Spirit. This life is one of intimate communion with God in Christ" (*Reformed Dogmatics*, 519).

25. Bavinck indicates our regeneration is always "a work of God by which a person is inwardly changed and renewed. This change is signified and sealed in baptism." See Bavinck, *Reformed Dogmatics*, 508–9, and his whole chapter on "Calling and Regeneration," 504–22.

26. Calvin, *Institutes* 3.2.33.

27. Barth, *CD* IV/2, 522. Cf. John Thompson, *The Holy Spirit in the Theology of Karl Barth*, Princeton Theological Monograph Series (Pittsburgh: Pickwick Publications, 1991), ch. 6, "The Holy Spirit and the Church."

28. Barth, *CD* IV/2, 523. Barth's views of the covenant can be found in Arthur C. Cochrane, "Karl Barth's Doctrine of the Covenant," in *Major Themes in the Reformed Tradition*,

ed. Donald K. McKim, rpt. (Eugene, OR: Wipf & Stock Publishers, 1998),108–16.

29. On baptism see Geoffrey W. Bromiley, "The Meaning and Scope of Baptism," in *Major Themes in the Reformed Tradition*, ed. Donald K. McKim, rpt. (Eugene, OR: Wipf & Stock Publishers, 1998), 234–44.

30. Calvin, *Institutes* 4.14.6.

31. Ibid., 4.15.1.

32. Ibid., 4.17.1. A helpful study is Martha L. Moore-Keish, *Do This in Remembrance of Me: A Ritual Approach to Reformed Eucharistic Theology* (Grand Rapids: Eerdmans, 2008), as well as Robert M. Shelton, "A Theology of the Lord's Supper from the Perspective of the Reformed Tradition," in *Major Themes in the Reformed Tradition*, ed. Donald K. McKim, rpt. (Eugene, OR: Wipf & Stock Publishers, 1998), 259–70.

33. Calvin, *Institutes* 4.14.9.

34. Jürgen Moltmann, *The Spirit of Life: A Universal Affirmation*, trans. Margaret Kohl (Minneapolis: Fortress Press, 1992), 9. See Col. 1:15–20.

35. Ibid., 10.

36. Ibid.

37. *Book of Confessions* 10.4.

38. John Calvin, *The Epistles of Paul the Apostle to the Galatians, Ephesians, Philippians and Colossians*, trans. T. H. L. Parker, in *Calvin's New Testament Commentaries*, 12 vols., ed. David W. Torrance and Thomas F. Torrance, rpt. (Grand Rapids: Eerdmans, 1980), *Commentary on Galatians 5:25* (CNTC 11:106).

Chapter 5: Ministry in Today's Cultures

1. T. W. Manson, *The Church's Ministry* (London: Hodder & Stoughton, 1948), 21, 24.

2. Richard J. Neuhaus, *Freedom for Ministry* (San Francisco: Harper & Row, 1979), 35.

3. Ibid. In the Reformed tradition, both clergy and laity carry out ministries.

4. Paul Minear, *Images of the Church in the New Testament*, rpt. (Louisville, KY: Westminster John Knox Press, 2004).

5. See Ephesians 1:22; 4:15; 5:23; Col. 1:18; 2:19. On Jesus Christ as the "head of the church," see Eph. 1:23; 2:16; 4:4, 12, 16; 6:23, 30; Col. 1:18, 22, 24; 2:19; 3:15.

6. Dietrich Bonhoeffer, *The Communion of Saints* (New York: Harper & Row, 1960), 85. Cf. 100ff., 135–36, 143, 145, and so on.

7. Ibid, 101.

8. Karl Barth, *Church Dogmatics*, IV/1, trans. G. W. Bromiley (New York: Charles Scribner's Sons, 1956), 661.

9. Robert S. Paul, *The Church in Search of Its Self* (Grand Rapids: Eerdmans, 1972), 39.

10. T. W. Manson, *Ministry and Priesthood: Christ's and Ours* (Richmond, VA: John Knox Press, 1959), 14.

11. See Matt. 4:23; 9:34; Luke 8:1; 9:11; cf. Luke 4:43–44. This is recognized by nearly all New Testament scholars and theologians. See *Interpreter's Dictionary of the Bible*, ed. George A. Buttrick, 4 vols. (New York: Abingdon Press,1962), 3:20, and Hans Küng, *On Being a Christian*, trans. Edward Quinn (New York: Doubleday, 1976), 214–25, 235–39, among a host of others.

12. See Presbyterian Church in the United States of America, The Constitution of the Presbyterian Church (U.S.A.), *Book of Order, 2011–2013* (Louisville, KY: Office of the General Assembly, 2011), *Directory for Worship* 4.4.003 i.(1) and (3) [p. 123].

13. See the essay by John Knox, "The Ministry in the Primitive Church," in *The Ministry in Historical Perspectives*, ed. H. Richard Niebuhr and Daniel D. Williams (New York: Harper & Brothers, 1956), 1–26, and Harry G. Goodykoontz, *The Minister in the Reformed Tradition* (Richmond, VA: John Knox Press, 1963), ch. 2.

14. See J. C. Hoekendijk, *The Church Inside Out*, trans. Isaac C. Rottenberg, ed. L. A. Hoedemaker and Pieter Tijmes (Philadelphia: Westminster Press, 1966); Karl Barth, *Church Dogmatics*, IV/2, trans. G.W. Bromiley, rpt. (Edinburgh: T.&T. Clark, 1967), 690ff.; Robert S. Paul, *Ministry* (Grand

Rapids: Eerdmans, 1965); Avery Dulles, *Models of the Church* (New York: Doubleday Image Books, 1978), ch. 6, "The Church as Servant." Other writers supporting this view are Claude Welch, *The Reality of the Church* (New York: Charles Scribner's Sons, 1958), part 3: "The Form of the Servant"; Colin W. Williams, *The Church*, New Directions in Theology Today, vol. 4 (Philadelphia: Westminster Press, 1968), ch. 6; Hans Küng, *The Church*, trans. Ray and Rosalee Ockenden (New York: Sheed and Ward, 1967), 388ff.; T. W. Manson, John Knox, and John L. McKenzie, *Authority in the Church* (New York: Doubleday Image Books, 1971). McKenzie contends the full force of *diakonos* is lost in English when it is merely rendered as "service." He writes that the term means "a lackey, a menial" (23–24).

15. Küng, *The Church*, 392. Cf. Küng, *On Being a Christian*, 486. Cf. Mark 10:45; Matt. 20:28; 23:6–11; John 12:25–26.

16. Paul, *Church in Search of Its Self*, 297.

17. The Presbyterian Church (U.S.A.), *Book of Confessions: Study Edition* (Louisville, KY: Geneva Press, 1999), 9.06. Karl Barth wrote that "the doctrine of reconciliation is itself the first or last or central word in the whole Christian confession or the whole of Christian dogma. Dogmatics has no more exalted or profound word—essentially, indeed, it has no other word—than this: that God was in Christ reconciling the world unto Himself (2 Cor. 5:19)." See Karl Barth, *Church Dogmatics*, II/2, trans. G.W. Bromiley, *et.al.*, rpt. (Edinburgh: T. & T. Clark, 1967), 88. Barth develops the doctrine of reconciliation in volume 4 of his *Church Dogmatics*. To see reconciliation in relation to the church, see the fine study by Kimlyn J. Bender, *Karl Barth's Christological Ecclesiology*, rpt. (Eugene, OR: Wipf & Stock Publishers, 2013), especially chapter 5: "Reconciliation as the Context of Ecclesiology."

18. Neuhaus, *Freedom for Ministry*, 67–68. Cf. his section, "Conforming and Transforming," 67–70.

19. Calvin, *Institutes* 3.2.42, 43.

20. Barth, *Church Dogmatics* IV/3/2, trans. G.W. Bromiley, rpt. (Edinburgh: T.&T. Clark, 1992), 915.

21. Ibid., 916.

Chapter 6: What It Means to Be Reformed

1. William Perkins, "A Golden Chaine: or, The Description of Theologie," in *The Workes of That Famous and Worthy Minister of Christ in the University of Cambridge, Mr. William Perkins*, 3 vols. (Cambridge: John Legatt, 1616–18), 1:11.

2. John Calvin, *Institutes of the Christian Religion* 3.2.36, ed. John T. McNeill, trans. Ford Lewis Battles, LCC (Philadelphia: Westminster Press, 1960), 583.

3. Presbyterian Church (U.S.A.), *Book of Confessions: Study Edition* (Louisville, KY: Geneva Press, 1996), 5.001, 5.002.

4. Presbyterian Church (U.S.A.), "The Nature of Revelation in the Christian Tradition from a Reformed Perspective," 199th General Assembly (1987), 28.205, in *Major Themes in the Reformed Tradition*, ed. Donald K. McKim, rpt. (Eugene, OR: Wipf & Stock, 1998), 43.

5. Karl Barth, *Church Dogmatics*, I/1, ed. G. W. Bromiley and T. F. Torrance, trans. G. W. Bromiley, rpt. (Edinburgh: T. & T. Clark, 1980), 321.

6. Presbyterian Church (U.S.A.), "The Nature of Revelation," 28.215, in *Major Themes*, 45.

7. *Book of Confessions* 6.002.

8. Ibid., 1.1.

9. Hendrikus Berkhof, *Christian Faith*, rev. ed., trans. Sierd Woudstra (Grand Rapids: Eerdmans, 1986), 157.

10. Ibid., 159.

11. Calvin, *Institutes* 1.2.1. Cf. 1.2.2: God is "the fountainhead and source of every good."

12. See Daniel L. Migliore, *Faith Seeking Understanding: An Introduction to Christian Theology*, 2nd ed. (Grand Rapids: Eerdmans, 2004), 92–96.

13. See Berkhof, *Christian Faith*, 166–67.

14. Calvin, *Institutes* 2.1.9.

15. Ibid. Later Reformed theologians spoke of humans as existing in "total depravity," meaning that sin affects the totality of human existence—all dimensions.

16. Karl Barth, *Church Dogmatics*, I/2, ed. G. W. Bromiley and T. F. Torrance, trans. G. T. Thomson and Harold Knight, rpt. (Edinburgh: T. & T. Clark, 1963), 123.

17. Calvin, *Institutes* 2.6.4.
18. *Book of Confessions* 10.2.
19. "The First Helvetic Confession of 1536," in *Reformed Confessions of the Sixteenth Century*, ed. Arthur C. Cochrane, with a new introduction by Jack Rogers (Louisville, KY: Westminster John Knox Press, 2003), 103 [Article 11].
20. Migliore, *Faith Seeking Understanding*, 177.
21. Ibid., 178.
22. This stems from Calvin's explication in *Institutes* 2.15.
23. Ibid., 2.15.1–2.
24. Ibid., 2.15.4.
25. Ibid., 2.15.6.
26. Ibid., 2.16.4.
27. Ibid., 2.16.3.
28. Karl Barth, *Church Dogmatics*, IV/1, ed. G. W. Bromiley and T. F. Torrance, trans. G. W. Bromiley (Edinburgh: T. & T. Clark, 1956), 309. (Hereafter referred to as *CD*.)
29. Calvin, *Institutes* 2.16.13. Barth wrote that "the death and resurrection of Jesus Christ are together—His death in the power and effectiveness and truth and lasting newness given to it by His resurrection—the basis of the alteration of the situation of men of all times" (*CD* IV/1, 316).
30. *Book of Confessions* 10.2.
31. Karl Barth, *Church Dogmatics*, II/2, ed. G. W. Bromiley and T. F. Torrance, trans. G. W. Bromiley et al., rpt. (Edinburgh: T. & T. Clark, 1967), 513.
32. Calvin, *Institutes* 3.2.2.
33. Ibid., 3.22.9.
34. Ibid., 3.22.10.
35. Ibid., 3.24.1.
36. Ibid., 3.24.4.
37. Ibid.
38. Ibid., 3.24.5.
39. Ibid., 3.24.6.
40. Ibid., 4.1.7.
41. *Book of Confessions* 9.31.
42. The Constitution of the Presbyterian Church (U.S.A.), *Book of Order, 2011–2013* (Louisville, KY: Office of the General Assembly, 2011), "The Mission of the Church," F-1.01.

A contemporary emphasis among a number of Reformed theologians and in some Reformed denominations is on the "missional church," which means mission is seen as "not merely an activity of the church. Rather, mission is the result of God's initiative, rooted in God's purpose to restore and heal creation." Here, "the mission of God (*missio Dei*)" is understood as "the foundation for the mission of the church. The church [is defined] as the community spawned by the mission of God and gathered up into that mission. The church [understands] that in any place it is a community sent by God. 'Mission' is not something the church does, a part of its total program. No, the church's essence is missional, for the calling and sending action of God forms its identity. Mission is founded on the mission of God in the world, rather than the church's effort to extend itself." See *Missional Church: A Vision for the Sending of the Church in North America*, ed. Darrell L. Guder (Grand Rapids: Eerdmans, 1998), 4, 81–82. Theological foundations for the church's mission and ministry are explored in Donald K. McKim, "A Reformed Perspective on the Mission of the Church in Society" in *Major Themes in the Reformed Tradition*, ed. Donald K. McKim, rpt. (Eugene, OR: Wipf & Stock, 1998), 361–71.

43. *Book of Confessions* 9.48. See 9.48–52.

44. Calvin, *Institutes* 4.1.9.

45. Migliore, *Faith Seeking Understanding*, 234.

46. See my "The 'Call' in the Reformed Tradition," in *Major Themes in the Reformed Tradition*, 335-43.

47. *Book of Confessions* 9.55.

SUGGESTIONS FOR FURTHER STUDY

In addition to works cited in the notes, the following resources are helpful:

Allen, R. Michael. *Reformed Theology. Doing Theology.* New York: T. & T. Clark International, 2010.

Bierma, Lyle D. *The Theology of the Heidelberg Catechism: A Reformation Synthesis.* Columbia Series in Reformed Theology. Louisville, KY: Westminster John Knox Press, 2013.

Elwood, Christopher. *Calvin for Armchair Theologians.* Louisville, KY: Westminster John Knox Press, 2002.

Guthrie, Shirley C., Jr. *Always Being Reformed: Faith for a Fragmented World.* 2nd ed. Louisville, KY: Westminster John Knox Press, 2008.

Hart, D. G. *Calvinism: A History.* New Haven, CT: Yale University Press, 2013.

McKim, Donald K. *Introducing the Reformed Faith: Biblical Revelation, Christian Tradition, Contemporary Significance.* Louisville, KY: Westminster John Knox Press, 2001.

———. *More Presbyterian Questions, More Presbyterian Answers: Exploring Christian Faith.* Louisville, KY: Geneva Press, 2011.

———. *Presbyterian Beliefs: A Brief Introduction.* Louisville, KY: Geneva Press, 2003.

———. *Presbyterian Questions, Presbyterian Answers: Exploring Christian Faith.* Louisville, KY: Geneva Press, 2003.

Pauw, Amy Plantinga, and Serene Jones, eds. *Feminist and Womanist Essays in Reformed Dogmatics.* Columbia Series in Reformed Theology. Louisville, KY: Westminster John Knox Press, 2005.

Small, Joseph D., ed. *Conversations with the Confessions: Dialogue in the Reformed Tradition.* Louisville, KY: Geneva Press, 2005.

CPSIA information can be obtained
at www.ICGtesting.com
Printed in the USA
FFOW01n0914040317
33099FF